Association for Middle Level Education

Managing the madness

A Practical Guide to Understanding Young Adolescents & Classroom Management

Jack C. Berckemeyer

Printed in the United States of America.

ISBN 978-1-56090-291-1

Library of Congress Cataloging-in-Publication Data

Names: Berckemeyer, Jack C., author.
Title: Managing the madness : a practical guide to understanding young adolescents & classroom management / Jack C. Berckemeyer.
Description: Westerville : Association for Middle Level Education, 2018.
Identifiers: LCCN 2017041706 (print) | LCCN 2017042586 (ebook) | ISBN 9781560902928 (ebook) | ISBN 9781560902911 (978-1-56090-291-1)
Subjects: LCSH: Middle school teaching--United States. | High school teaching--United States. | Classroom management--United States.
Classification: LCC LB1623.5 (ebook) | LCC LB1623.5 .B47 2018 (print) | DDC 373.1102--dc23
LC record available at https://lccn.loc.gov/2017041706

Association for Middle Level Education
4151 Executive Parkway, Suite 300
Westerville, Ohio 43081 | amle.org

Foreword

Wow, Jack Berckemeyer is back, and he's more Jack-ian than ever! Yes, he's written several books since he wrote the first version of *Managing the Madness*, but here he returns to the gold that makes Jack Jack. We could say this content has been revised, but it wouldn't do justice to what's truly offered here. The man is on fire with new insights, deeper diving, candid commentary, provocative research, instructional versatility, and edgy humor. There is some serious evolution in Jack's thinking here, too; all of it impressive, all of it useful.

If we're honest, there are moments with Jack when we think we're in the presence of absolute genius; he's a dynamo that never fails to inspire. Using everyday classroom realities, Jack cultivates our instructional potential, using acts of kindness, stunning wit, and vibrant applications of the middle level concept. And just as refreshing, there are other times when Jack is an overgrown adolescent who is making good on his promise to his teachers that he'd one day rule the educational universe and inject it with a healthy dose of warped and wonderful humor. We are lucky to be in his orbit.

Jack gives the latest research in teaching young adolescents life skills through his large repertoire of personal anecdotes, uncanny comprehension of student and teacher psychology, and real-teaching savvy. He is up there with John Lounsbury, Nancy Doda, and Paul George as a consummate ambassador for middle level education. I've never seen someone wed the big ideas of education with their requisite details so skillfully and compel us to do the same.

In this new version of *Managing the Madness*, we, "Release the Berckemeyer!" As we unfold Jack's turbo-powered teaching acumen, we find innovative and specific ideas on discipline, humor, integration, seating arrangements, student-teacher interaction, bulletin boards, attention grabbers, classroom management, and much more. He tackles the most awkward situations that arise in middle level classrooms that are not often considered in other books. Seriously, he's education's, *Pragmatist Whisperer*, providing savvy responses to daily issues in teaching and multiple avenues to students' hearts and minds. His ideas here are full of, "Why didn't we think of that?" common sense, but he also pushes us to color outside the lines, and our teacher's craft is all the more beautiful for it. Dang, I wish I taught next door to him, or had him as my own teacher!

The samples, forms, and, "Reflection and Action," sections are compelling and helpful, but Jack has taken his research, humor, candor, and practical sense to new levels as well. His writing crackles as he writes about developing students' social skills, classroom management tips, parents, bullying, technology, and real-world importance of students learning to interact with adults and each other with civility. It's a stunning maturation from the first book. This revised version will be among the first books I give to new teachers and to seasoned education colleagues I respect.

Many of the legendary stories that Jack shares in his training sessions are included here along with new ones that reflect the modern world. His unique voice comes through every word. I lost count of the number of times I nodded in agreement and laughed aloud while reading these ideas. How does this man get inside the minds of young adolescents so well and tell their truth so powerfully? And how does he do the same with the adults who guide them? Jack operates daily on a wavelength many of us can only dream of experiencing.

Through this book, let's bring Jack to each team meeting, give him to colleagues in need of hope and creativity, and use his wisdom to feed our teaching souls. Let's share him, too, with our students' parents who aren't sure what to do with this morphing middle schooler under their roof. There's plenty of humanity here alongside the demonstrated professionalism to help all those with skin in the game.

And particularly resonant with many of us, Jack demonstrates the people and pedagogy connections that help us reach increasingly diverse adolescents and just as importantly, to stay in the profession. We have no choice but to teach like today is the only day we get with our students; every moment counts. Let's enjoy where Jack places us—in the driver's seat of the school bus—while he rides in the back, grinning and bouncing high as he teaches us with every bump of the road. Jack is the mad scientist (Boo-Ha-Ha!) at work.

No signed permission slip needed: This is a trip every middle level teacher should take as often as possible, and with every new turn of road.

—Rick Wormeli

Rick is a teacher trainer, columnist for *AMLE Magazine*, and author of the books *Meet Me in the Middle: Becoming an Accomplished Middle Level Teacher*, *Day One and Beyond: Practical Matters for New Middle Level Teachers*, *Summarization in any Subject*, *Fair Isn't Always Equal: Assessing & Grading in the Differentiated Classroom*, *Differentiation: From Planning to Practice*, *Metaphors & Analogies: Power Tools for Teaching any Subject*, and *The Collected Writings (So Far) of Rick Wormeli*, and of the video series "At Work in the Differentiated Classroom."

Contents

Foreword by Rick Wormeli i

My Thanks & Appreciation v

It's True, Honest!. vii

Chapter 1   What Madness? 1

Chapter 2   Why They Run Into Walls. 7

Chapter 3   A Place Where They Want to Be 29

Chapter 4   More Engagement, Less Madness 45

Chapter 5   Of Manners and Other Social Skills 77

Chapter 6   Getting Ahead of the Madness 99

Chapter 7   Intervention That Works. 119

Chapter 8   The Power of Their Power 141

Chapter 9   Living the Dream. 165

Appendix
    A   Characteristics and Needs of Young Adolescents. 169
    B   Resources Cited and Recommended. 176

About the Author 181

My Thanks & Appreciation

Creating this book was truly a journey for me. Because there are so few times one can thank people who have positively influenced my life, (and who knows how many books I'll be fortunate or mentally competent enough to write?)—I thank those who pushed me, encouraged me, and made me sound so wonderful. This includes Marj Frank, Pete Lorain, Kathy Hunt-Ullock, and Sue Swaim; your wisdom, advice, and mentoring have made me a better educator and person.

To my past teammates at Scott Carpenter: thanks for making me laugh every day. A big thanks to goes to Jan Blatchford, Zerphayne Willis, Annette Fante, and Susie DeSmit for your support and friendship.

Thanks to Patricia Yellico, Tina Cerventes, Tom Dewar, and Roberta Fromhart for being the best middle school teachers a future educational speaker-humorist could ever have.

Finally, this book is dedicated to my parents, Jack and Sharon Berckemeyer, for paying for my college education and for your constant love and support. I am proud to be your son!

And to the teachers, administrators, and consultants with whom I have worked and who make a huge impact on the lives of young adolescents (and other students of all ages), I say, "Thanks!"

It's True, Honest!

Every educator has a story about how he or she got that first teaching job. Some simply applied, interviewed, and got the job; others spent hours researching the job market and filling out the vast pre-screening assessments that districts ask you to complete to make sure you are not a maniac of some sort. Some just looked in their own home-towns and found the perfect job; others sought adventure and followed the appeal of working in an international school—exploring the delights and challenges of moving halfway around the world.

My journey was unique; I did not venture out into new continents or even find a job in my hometown. In fact, I was hired to teach right out of college and right in the middle of the school year.

I had just finished my student teaching. Out of the blue, I got a call from Scott Carpenter Middle School in Adams County School District, Denver, Colorado. At the time, like so many struggling new teachers, I lived in my parents' basement, which was about 60 miles away in Colorado Springs. I had planned on substitute teaching while I searched for a job very close to home for the next school year. Even though I'd grown up overseas and thought of myself as an adventuresome soul, I wanted to be close to home.

I moved around a lot as a child. This gave me the desire to find permanent roots and stay closer to family and friends.

My parents moved to Colorado Springs when I was in eighth grade. It was the first time I truly felt at home. Looking back, I believe this had a lot to do with being in a small school district (Falcon) where I felt safe even though I had to ride the bus ten miles to school in a rural part of the state. With only 85 kids in my graduating class, I became comfortable with a smaller school and district. In my wildest dreams, I never thought I would get a job—or want a job—in the big, bad city of Denver.

Much to my own surprise, I took the opportunity to be interviewed. As was typical in those days, eight people took part in the conversation (or examination, so it felt); three of them were my future teammates. In addition, the principal, assistant principal, and the guidance counselor joined us. There they sat, my future teammates—my potential support system: Ms. Tossava, who taught social studies, Ms. Trumbo, the best special education teacher ever, and a gentleman by the name of Mr. Gassman, who taught science. (What kind of middle school teacher has the name Gassman?) I always made sure I pronounced his name with an extra special emphasis on each part of his name—Gas Man. It was a joy to work with all of them; their humor and caring made my first year a success.

If you've met me or heard me speak, you know that humor is a fundamental part of my life. I grew up with laughter and formed most of my quality relationships based on love and laughter. So I was pleased when it became apparent during the interview that if I got the job, humor would play a huge part in our team's dynamics.

The interview was going along smoothly until, while I was answering a question enthusiastically, a big drop of spit flew out of my mouth and landed well toward the middle of the table. (When I get excited, spit comes out.) So, as the spit gleamed on the table, everyone started looking at the spit and not at me. Feeling that I had lost all control of the interview, I did what any good teacher would do. I diverted their attention by putting my hand over the spit. Then, further excited (or nervous?), I inadvertently pulled my hand back, smearing the spit. The important point, however, is: I got the job—along with questioning looks and laughter from my principal, future teammates, and the counselor, who, I had figured out by then, was present to assist me should I suffer a nervous breakdown.

So now I had the job. "What next?" I wondered. Well, the next step was a meeting with the principal. He informed me that I would get my own classroom, which was a perk because our school was overcrowded and some of the teachers (we called them "teachers on a cart") pushed carts from room to room like vagabonds. I was thrilled not to be pushing a cart or sharing a room with another teacher. We all know how territorial teachers can be!

Next, the principal let me know that I'd be teaching an "elective exploratory" class along with my regular language arts and social studies classes. That sounded exciting! When I inquired what the elective would be, he answered that it would be an eighth-grade language arts class. Now, I know you are wondering the same thing that I asked: "Since when is eighth grade language arts an elective?"

Then it came—one of those answers for educators to beware. The principal responded, "They are a unique group of kids." He mentioned, rather offhandedly, that about half the students were gifted and talented, and the other half had criminal records.

During that first semester teaching the eighth grade language arts "exploratory" class, I found that I could not tell which students were the criminals and which were gifted. Because I was hired in the middle of the year, teachers from the other teams chose which of their students to give to me. You can imagine the types of students I was blessed to receive! Combine the unique group dynamics of the class with the fact that I was a new teacher who had started in the middle of the year, and you can imagine my trepidations! I knew that I had to start off with a bang and lay down the law right away.

> When I'm Ruler of Education, "electives" will be called "essentials." The topics students explore and learn in these classes are absolutely essential to their growth and development.

As you can see, my first year of teaching was not even close to textbook perfect. I wish I could say I relied on all the textbook knowledge from college. Granted, it certainly helped some. Far more important to my success that year was a combination of other factors: likeable, clever students; good mentors; outstanding colleagues and mentors; a supportive team; patient-with-me parents; and a music, P.E., and art teacher who supported me nonstop. Thank you, Ms. Blatchford, Ms. Willis, and Mrs. DeSmit. Looking back, I realize how much my ability and willingness to reach out for help and listen to others also contributed to my survival! So did my sense of humor and dedication to teaching young adolescents.

But perhaps what *really* saved me was my good fortune to be able to establish a strong sense of classroom management based on consistency, respect, and the ability to listen and laugh every day. I am forever thankful for those colleagues who mentored me and helped me build a successful approach to classroom management. I have never forgotten the lifeline this gave me. And never since that first year have I underestimated the importance of thoughtful, well-planned, consistent proactive management.

CHAPTER 1

What Madness?

Mr. Berckemeyer, I got a cool collection of cicadas off the tree in front of my house this morning—right here in this lunch bag! I promise I'll keep them in my backpack.

If you teach young adolescents, the above question immediately sparks concrete, visual images. When you walk into a middle level classroom, you see:

- All different sizes and shapes of bodies in an amazing assortment of well-chosen (or poorly-chosen) outfits.

- An assortment of maturation levels—physical, cognitive, emotional, and social.

- Fast-growing, fast-changing beings—part child, part adult.

- Activity levels ranging from non-stop motion and chattering (squirrels on amphetamines) to lethargy and apathy or downright falling asleep (sluggish bears on Ambien®)—and that's just within ONE kid!

- A mass of actions, issues, and attitudes from wildness to seriousness to boredom to eagerness to curiosity to skepticism to whining to drama to brilliance to hilarity.

- An ambiance of wisecracks, crack-up humor, odors, and startling wisdom.

For one thing, this classroom is never a dull place! It's wonderful, frightening, energizing, frustrating, delightful, surprising, and full of pitfalls and possibilities—but never dull! Did you want dull? Calm? Orderly? Ooops, you chose the wrong grade level! Whatever were you thinking?

Manage This?

"So, Jack," you ask, "you're saying I can manage this madness?" Yes! And, guess what? It is not a terrifying, horrible chore (well, not as often as you might fear). Okay, it's a challenge. But if you're working at this level, undoubtedly you already are brave (or emotionally unbalanced). And you already believe in kids this age and even want to be with them and probably—albeit perhaps secretly—enjoy them!

Yes, you can have a classroom that your students and you look forward to entering. Because, you know what? As you might have picked up from my descriptions above, the "madness" is not a negative scenario. It's an awesome, dynamic bedlam that you can manage. And when well managed, the madness leads to caring relationships, a safe environment, superb creative accomplishments, top-notch learning experiences, heightened achievement, and a whole lot of fun for you and your students.

You'll notice my deep love of middle level education and middle level students, and my long-time work in generating passion and superb teaching for this developmental level. In this book, I will often refer to "young adolescents." Because of the erratic nature of students' development in late elementary and post elementary grades, this term applies to a wide range of grade levels and ages (generally ages 10 to 15). Yet, even older adolescents have many of the same developmental characteristics as the group we've long referred to as "middle level." Because of this, the strategies and suggestions in this book are applicable to grade levels below and above official middle school grades—well into high school. My zeal for education that is geared to students' developmental characteristics and my work with students and educators, as well, extend to all grade levels.

How to Manage?

Now, colleges and universities do try conscientiously to prepare fledgling teachers to manage classrooms well. However, clearly this is one area of the profession that has to be learned and honed through a multitude of experiences. Successful management comes through patience and practice. Some of it is about trial and error. (Some seems to come from sheer, dumb luck!)

But, it's not just "feeling your way along"—not at all. Managing the madness of living and learning with young adolescents is greatly assisted by teamwork with colleagues, quality mentoring, paying attention to good advice and examples from multiple sources, willingness to seek help when needed, and *certainly* from thoughtful planning. And a huge dose of humor is an *absolutely crucial ingredient*.

For a long time I have had this dream that I would become the Ruler of Education. Not Secretary of Education—but Ruler! When I am Ruler of Education, I'll be able to issue edicts about what should happen. I share this dream often at conferences and workshops. One workshop participant shot up her hand and spoke out, "I'd vote for you for this position, Jack."

I had to clarify the dream for her. "You don't understand. When I am Ruler of Education, you don't get to vote!"

> When I'm Ruler of Education, teachers-to-be will be required to demonstrate proficient classroom management skills before earning a certificate.

The following chapters offer thoughts, hard-learned lessons, tried and tested ideas, and practical advice for some thoughtful ways to manage that madness. In my experience, this important task includes:

- Knowing who your students are (their development, needs, culture, quirks, pressures, interests, fears, fads, and individual personalities and situations).

- Creating a physical, emotional, and social environment that is safe, caring, and stimulating enough for them to get along with each other, learn, and flourish.

- Filling their time with relevant, important, dynamic, challenging, and *downright engaging* activities suitable for their developmental and academic needs.

- Teaching and modeling social skills and proper behavior, not just in the beginning, but every day.

- Learning and reinforcing proactive, rather than reactive, management practices that avoid, divert, lessen, and handle common problems, disruptions, and issues.

- Having a thoughtful and workable intervention plan for students who can't, won't, or don't hold to the general procedures or find success with academic or behavioral expectations—a plan that gets all the adults together with a student to caringly and expertly help her or him make progress in a positive direction.

- Harnessing and channeling the wonderful gift of adolescent power, giving honor and attention to students' voices, and holding them accountable for their possibilities and actions.

Although individual chapters focus on each of the above topics, you'll find that similar beliefs, attitudes, themes, concepts, and advice infuse all the chapters. You'll see such words and phrases as *respect, relationships, student voice, student choice, engagement, clear expectations, protocols, humor, follow-through, accountability, trust,* and *affirmation* again and again!

Every chapter ends with a chance for you to pause and reflect on the ideas. Questions and suggestions on a page titled: "For Reflection and Action" prompt you to review your current practices, consider what suggestions can work for you, set goals, and try out some new practices.

All of these components lead to managing in a way that diminishes or derails many issues and makes the madness productive and way more than tolerable—enjoyable, actually!

Do It Your Way

In this book, I've not suggested one solution or type of solution for all situations. This is a free-flowing discussion of ideas based on my observations and experiences helping teachers (including myself) get through daily rounds of uprisings, hostage situations (with demands), commotions, and chaos. *(Please note that some of my examples are really humorous asides and should not be taken literally.)*

Readers will readily realize that the book's strategies reflect my personality. I encourage you to discern which ideas fit comfortably with your personality and teaching style. Never try to be someone you are not in the classroom. Modify any of these suggestions to fit your personal style, tolerance levels, classroom, and students. Practice patience. Seek out excellent seasoned teachers who can share a wealth of knowledge. Try new things that you see work for others or good ideas you find in books or other resources. Here are a few of my favorites: *If You Can't Manage Them, you Can't Teach Them* (Campbell, 2012), *Fires in the Bathroom: Advice for Teachers from High School Students* (Cushman, 2003), and *Fires in the Middle School Bathroom: Advice for Teachers from Middle Schoolers* (Cushman & Rogers, 2009). Trust your own instincts. Listen to your students; you'll probably learn the most from them about what works and what doesn't!

If a team, department, study group, or an entire faculty reads this book at the same time, look for solutions the whole team or all teams can implement and accomplish as a unit.

Most important—have some fun along the way. School is a serious place for learning, but it can also be a place filled with humor and laughter. You'll find more about humor later in this book. I also recommend you pursue some resources on adding humor to your classroom. One good source is Lee Hurren's book *Humor in School Is Serious Business* (2010). It gives practical help for teachers at any grade level—even those who are not natural comedians!

All too often, the art of humor has been lost or intentionally discouraged from classrooms and schools. Educators feel an immense amount of pressure, which lowers teacher morale and drains fun and humor. When an educator suffers from low morale, discipline conflicts arise and students and teachers in any class suffer from diminished joy in their school lives. There is nothing more powerful than a classroom with a joyful educator: discipline problems decrease, achievement rises, students have better attitudes, and overall morale increases. Give your students the gifts of joy and humor. You'll want to come to school, and so will they. And when you all get there, the operation of the classroom will be much smoother.

For Reflection and Action

1. What does the madness look like in your classroom?

2. What benefits, positives, or possibilities can you see in the madness?

3. Identify some of your current management strategies that are working well to channel the madness. Capitalize on and expand those.

4. Find a time to ask your students for their ideas about what makes a classroom work, what helps them get along, what gets in the way of their learning, or what makes them feel safe, valued, and comfortable enough to do well. Make a list. Discuss it with students. Use it to set some goals for new strategies based on their ideas.

Source: *Managing the Madness: A Practical Guide to Understanding Young Adolescents and Classroom Management*
© Association for Middle Level Education   www.amle.org

CHAPTER 2

Why They Run Into Walls

Mr. Berckemeyer, this time I promise to ask a meaningful question.

Breanna was just one of many students who constantly asked questions—irrelevant, vague, off-topic questions—often in a tone of voice that had a bit of desperation. I would have welcomed just one *meaningful* question from her! I came to recognize this tactic early in my teaching career. These questioners don't want answers; they want you, and perhaps their classmates too, to *see* them, notice they exist, be interested in them, hear their voices, or pay attention. Sometimes I'm convinced that they also want to hear their own voices—to reassure themselves that they are somebody!

Compulsive waving of the hands in the air and asking mostly dumb questions, annoying as it is, is a signal to the teacher. It's a reminder that every student needs and deserves to be seen, known, taken seriously, heard, and cared about.

James Comer is one of the world's leading child psychologists and long-time researcher of the conditions that foster academic success for students, including underprivileged children. This statement from him says it all—about all students: "No significant learning occurs without a significant relationship" (1995).

Dr. Comer's simple statement is backed by an ever-growing body of research that affirms the facts: in the presence of caring, trusting relationships, students are more at ease, feel better about themselves and about school, are less likely to have problems at school, get along better with each other, feel less lonely and depressed, are more engaged in learning activities, and achieve at higher academic levels.

Sadly, in many schools (and particularly beyond elementary school) there are students sitting at desks and wandering the halls who don't have even one constant significant relationship with an adult at the school. Hopefully, each of your students has more than one. But don't count on it. Take it upon yourself (and within your team or grade level group) to make sure that *every single* one of your students is sure you are there for him or her.

These students may look like adults or almost-adults; they may talk tough, act distant, roll their eyes at things you say, and feign total independence. *Don't be fooled.* Young adolescents desperately need to feel that you know them, want to be with them, believe in them, and have their backs.

Knowing your students and connecting with them is a major foundation for good classroom management. You'll be up a creek if you try to reach goals of organizing a classroom, increasing academic success, and enhancing acceptable behavior without building this foundation!

According to Steven Wolk (2003), author of two books on democratic classroom management, classrooms need engaged learning and caring teacher-student relationships simultaneously. He says that teachers must "win their students' hearts while getting inside their students' heads" (p. 14). All the while you work at meaningful teaching, democratic classroom procedures, and relationships in general, work to win hearts one student at a time through individual personal relationships that are respectful and caring. In their 2003 meta-analysis of more than 100 studies on classroom management, researchers Robert J. Marzano, Jana S. Marzano, and Debra J. Pickering (2003) concluded that teachers who develop such relationships with students have fewer behavior problems and better academic performance in their classrooms than teachers who do not (pp. 41-64).

Plenty of resources are readily available to help you build trusting, caring relationships with students. This chapter addresses some of the tactics that I have found most successful for meeting this goal. They fall into these categories:

1. Paying attention to students' need for attention.

2. Honoring the magic of humor.

3. Knowing the students—individually, and as a developmental group (understanding their physical, cognitive, emotional, and social characteristics).

4. Knowing and respecting their youth culture (a huge part of who they are).

Pay Attention

"I need attention and I need it now!" Many of your students are screaming this—out loud or silently. Young adolescents look for attention from their peers, parents, and teachers. This may not be overt. You might teach a lesson and not have any arms waving to ask questions—relevant or irrelevant. But at the bell (just when you're looking for a coveted few minutes of personal peace), you find yourself surrounded by nine smiling students standing ready to critique your choice of clothing or initiate connection with other comments: "I don't like your sweater." "Those shoes are cool." "You need a new hairstyle." "You're my favorite teacher." "Why do you give us homework?"

How many times do you have to chase your students out of the room so you can get ready for the next class? They crave adult interaction. This is crucial to their development. Being around you affirms their beliefs, allows them to use humor, and makes them feel more mature. Perhaps most important, it helps them feel that they belong.

Your willingness to listen to young adolescents is key to your success as a teacher. Let students know that they are valued and don't be afraid to smile as you share the precious commodity of your time. Even though your time is always tight, sharing it is a treasured gift for the student who just needs some adult interaction. That student can *see* you are busy—that you're rushing to the bathroom or trying to grab a sip of your cold coffee. Just think how honored she or he must feel when you stop to relate! The benefits are priceless for the student and for you.

Here's one thing about the craving for attention: Attention is attention. Often, it doesn't matter if it's positive or negative. In fact, when a student has not had enough (or any) positive attention or is uncomfortable with positive attention, you can be sure that kid will go straight for the negative kind. Have you ever had your praise of a young adolescent backfire? "Gee, Jamie, I am so glad you finished that assignment." Looking right at you he says something like this: "It was way easy and stupid—anyone could have done it" or "Mr. Berckemeyer, you are such a dork. And you need a Tic-Tac®."

During this exchange you are thinking, "Wait a minute; I am trying to be nice. I am giving praise. I am acknowledging that he is doing a good job. And in return he is being rude and disrespectful." Sometimes students who are used to negative attention are naturally uncomfortable with genuine positive responses and will continue to look for negative attention.

Equally annoying are the students who practically beg to get your praise and positive attention. When a "perfect" student completes an assignment within five minutes of your giving it and gets in your face asking, "What can I do? What can I do now?" you think, "You can get out of my face and sit down."

And then there are others who have an over-the-top craving and literally become stalkers. It's constant: "Mr. Berckemeyer, is this good?" "Mr. Berckemeyer is this an A?" "Mr Berckemeyer do you like what I did?" (Translated: "Mr. Berckemeyer, do you like me? Am I worthwhile?")

You might be tempted to say: "Did I *not* say it was gooood? Did I *not* say it was good in class when you asked the first ten times, and when you asked me in the hallway every single break of the day? Now get out of my car!" Yikes! Some will follow you anywhere to get attention!

In such scenarios, your natural response is to feel combative. But because you realize that this is about the classic need for attention—you refrain from the emotional response. Instead of grabbing the impudent student by the collar, you look for your Tic Tacs®. Instead of saying what you're thinking to the annoying over-pleasing student, you suggest something productive for him to do next. Instead of the tirade ending with "Get out of my car," you gently open the door and send your stalker away with a gentle pat on the head and a cheerful "See you tomorrow!"

There's an unwritten rule that I've noticed: we educators spend about 95% of our time dealing with 5% of the student population. It's frustrating and overwhelming. We need to be aware of this and develop strategies to wean some of our students away from constant attention seeking and nudge them toward self-sufficiency and self-affirmation. Showing students you truly are interested in them, along with thoughtful affirmation and encouragement, can help make strides toward these goals.

Here are some bits of wisdom I've learned about giving students affirmation and attention:

- There are times you feel you just have to jump up on a chair and shout out loud about how awesome a student's work sample is. But first, stop and think about what you know of the particular student. For some, that would be threatening, embarrassing, or overwhelming.

- Make sure you get students' permission before you use their work. Some might not feel comfortable with you sharing their thoughts, ideas, or feelings.

- Praise judiciously. While praise can be good for self-esteem, it is not all successful or healthy. Praise can embarrass some kids. It can turn others into praise junkies—committed to needing the teacher's approval and unable to find self-approval.

- Don't be on praise autopilot. If you walk around kids' desks passing out "good job," "well done," and "nice work" comments left and right, the praise may sound insincere (even if it's not). They'll stop believing you.

- Praise students for accomplishments—not for ability or intelligence.

- Affirm students with specific feedback. Tell something brief about the work—like that you see they've mastered a skill or process: "You got it! Put a notch on your belt for multiplying with exponents," or "I can tell you understand this," or "Wow! That diagram helps me understand the rock cycle in an instant," or "Yikes! Your opening paragraph makes the hair on my neck stand up. I can't wait to see what comes next!"

- For students who are uncomfortable with affirmation, you might just make eye contact and say in a low voice, "That idea worked out well" or "You worked hard on this. It's paid off!" Next time you might give a low-key high five or pat on the back. Even better, wait until the end of class, call the student over, and make a comment about what was accomplished.

- For many students, the affirmation might be a warm, comforting smile or a slight head nod. Use the student's name in an example. Have the student share an answer with the class or demonstrate something he or she has mastered.

- Here are some other affirmative, encouraging tactics to use often: wink, give thumbs up, say something to make them smile or laugh, ask them to explain to you something in their work or teach you something, thank them for a behavior, or let them know you realize the work was a challenge and that they were up to it.

- To keep students from dependence on your approval and move toward the importance of their own approval, replace "I'm so proud of you" after an accomplishment with "You must be really proud of yourself" or "Tell me what makes you proud of this."

- Make this a habit: *at least once a week*, be sure to say something positive to every student as you walk around the room. Each one deserves a teacher who will provide him or her with encouraging, affirming feedback.

- Sharing their work and voicing their thoughts, discoveries, and questions— these things also help satisfy students' needs for connection and attention.

- Devise lessons that use their communication or reflection skills: cooperative group experiences, writing journals, or creation of digital messages, blogs, posts, and podcasts. These activities give students opportunities to express themselves, to raise issues and topics important to them, to receive feedback on their ideas and opinions, and to give feedback to others. Such lessons spill over into ongoing classroom discussions—allowing students more chances to give attention to one another, to learn about and value one another, and to affirm one another.

- Definitely read Debbie Silver's book, *Fall Down 7 Times, Get Up 8: Teaching Kids to Succeed* (2012). It is full of strategies for helping students develop internal motivation and productive habits.

The next time a student asks you a question such as "What are we doing today?" or "Are we doing anything fun?" or "Where is the homework basket?" or "What's wrong with the pencil sharpener?" or "Why do we have to do this?" remember that in many cases the student knows the answer to the question. What is sought, rather than an answer, is attention—yours, their classmates', or both. The intention is not to drive you insane. (However, some days it is a short drive!)

Embrace Humor

Here's a situation that you'll probably recognize; it happens often. The teacher is in one of her finest teaching moments animatedly explaining the solar system or how the earth is changing. And just when she has every student in the palm of her hand, some wise young adolescent makes a funny, but definitely inappropriate, comment.

In a science lesson of this sort, the comment usually involves one of the following words: *gas, balls,* or a reference to a planet that sounds like the word *anus.* While all the students laugh, the straight-faced teacher will say, "Nicolas, that is not funny." Meanwhile the teacher is thinking, "I need to write this down; they will so love this in the faculty lounge!"

Adolescent Humor

No subject or class is immune to the humor of young adolescents. Students pointing to a map and asking you the name of a lake can cause you to blush. But yes, you need to say "Lake Titicaca!" (However, with high school students, a story should never build to a "climax"! When teaching plot structure, you've got to figure out how to skirt around that one carefully.)

Young adolescents struggle with humor; they are not sure when it is appropriate to share their unique and often warped senses of humor. Sometimes, you wish they would struggle more—at least to put up some boundaries or think five seconds before it spills out of their mouths! As the teacher, you might struggle with knowing when it is okay to let down your guard and crack a smile. We fear letting things get too out-of-hand and losing control or risking that inappropriate stuff will reach the ears of other students. (And, of course, whatever humorous comments spill out during your class time will be texted to half the school before students even leave your room! And if you don't throw a hissy fit about the comments, the world will get the idea that you approved them—at least, that is what you fear!) However, some of the best advice you will ever receive about teaching young adolescents is to go ahead and enjoy their humor; it is okay to laugh. Just look at the way they interact with each other, not to mention what they say or their ever-changing hairstyles and colors! How can you not laugh?

Those of us who have dealt for a long time with unique and interesting students (a sweet way to describe young adolescents) realize the untruths we've been told. For example, "There is no such thing as a stupid question." How many of us get at least five stupid questions a day? Sometimes these off-the-wall questions come from students, sometimes from parents, and sometimes even from our colleagues. Humor helps us respond appropriately to unique opinions, bizarre statements, outlandish questions, and daily frustrations. Although teachers should never laugh *at* a student (this is ridicule), enjoying a good laugh *together* can be therapeutic for both you and students.

My motto is: if you do not laugh at least five times a day in a school, there is something wrong with you. Enjoy the ups and downs of working with your students; savor the roller coaster ride.

Here are some things I've learned about young adolescents and humor:

- Their own humor is ever-changing and evolving. It's always surprising!

- They can be sensitive regarding humor, sometimes intensely so. Build relationships with your students so you know what they can handle. Be considerate in using students' nicknames; use them only with each individual student's permission and when you are sure it is appropriate.

- Never take their humor personally. They can and do use humor to attack each other and even the teacher. When humor is rude or demeaning, address it right away. Don't laugh at it.

- Don't be afraid to laugh at yourself. When you do something funny or downright stupid, laugh about it.

- Students find nothing funnier than watching the teacher do something silly. Slapstick comedy works for young adolescents. This does not mean that you should light your tie or shirtsleeve on fire with the Bunsen burner—that is just scary and dangerous.

Student Stages of Humor

Remember that humor changes as kids grow. Elementary students love such jokes as this one:

What is green and hangs from trees?

Giraffe snot!

while older students think anything with a sexual connotation, body-part association, or bathroom connection is funny.

In developing their senses of humor, students typically start with simple jokes such as knock-knock jokes or one-liners they have read in a joke book or on the Internet. Some students won't "get" a joke and will need to have it explained. Before long—all too soon and increasingly at younger ages—kids will recognize that some jokes have negative or stereotypical punch lines. They'll also begin to pick up on sexual innuendos.

Then, as they progress to the next stages of humor, they will look for ways to embarrass and humiliate their peers, the teacher, or anyone close by. They find embarrassment funny, so they clap when someone drops a tray of food in the lunchroom or giggle when someone trips and falls. These are normal stages for most young adolescents. Understand that some might skip these stages or (even worse) get stuck in a certain stage for most of their adult lives. There are some adults who still laugh at certain words or bodily functions. Though they are legally adults, they struggle with moving beyond teenage humor into adult humor. (Do you know of an adult who still laughs at the words *gas* or *boobs*?)

A later stage of humor is the sarcasm stage—a tough stage to address. Sarcasm is often the lowest form of humor. By some definitions, sarcasm is a form of satire that uses an ironic statement to downplay the seriousness of something. But most uses of sarcasm are negative—even destructive.

Young adolescents and adolescents use sarcasm on a daily basis: they use it toward each other, toward teachers, toward schoolwork, and toward their parents. Theories abound that eighth-grade girls developed sarcasm. In fact, many of them use sarcasm (insults) wordlessly. All it takes is one look, a flick of the hair, or a wrinkled-up nose, and you know you have done something wrong or you are somehow flawed. Have you ever been on hall duty when an eighth-grade girl walked by and cut you down to size with a look, hair flick, or dagger stare that could cut glass? She might not even be aware of doing this; it's such a normal movement to her. Hopefully, many students will outgrow this adolescent sarcasm. (Unfortunately, many won't.)

Don't encourage sarcasm. In fact, find ways to let students know what sarcasm usually is: sharp use of words or nonverbal expressions to hurt someone. *Caustic, mocking, sneering, cutting, jeering,* or *derision* are parts of most dictionary definitions of the word. The intent is to insult or to wound. Perhaps sarcasm is a normal instinct; perhaps it is learned. But all the same, it is generally mean.

Other complex forms of humor such as irony and satire connect to real-life situations, have deeper meanings, or have multiple meanings. Can some young adolescents get to those stages? Yes, not many, but a few. Most have difficulty understanding deeper levels of humor so they may not laugh at something that seems extremely funny to you.

Teacher Humor

Humor belongs in every classroom. It builds class cohesion, spurs positive responses, relaxes and de-stresses students (and teacher), helps kids cope with stress, dissipates grumpiness, brings enthusiasm, and increases creativity and optimism. Students are more comfortable in classes where there is laughter. Perhaps most exciting: humor brings content to life. It keeps students engaged in the learning process and increases retention of material. A review of four decades of research on humor in education settings supports this well (Banas, Dunbar, Rodriguez, & Liu, 2011).

> Remember, anything is worth a try but you can only dress up and sing so many times in a year before your colleagues start to think that you have lost it and should retire early.

Humor grabs and sustains student interest. If you want students to get and remember an important concept, incorporate humor into the lesson. Appropriate use of humor can also help you build necessary connections with your students. It's an important part of the caring process. Expressing humor shows young adolescents that you like them and that you enjoy being around them. There's nothing quite so bonding as laughing together. So add your own teacher-initiated humor to your classroom, and welcome (and appreciate) appropriate insertions of student humor.

Some teachers are not comfortable with humor. Sometimes, school district officials ask me to teach their teachers to be funny. This is not an easy task. Some teachers are tied up so tightly that if they laugh, their bra straps or belts will shoot off and hurt someone. The truth is that almost everyone has a sense of humor. Everyone has the ability to laugh.

Every teacher does not have to be a natural stand-up comedian. Inevitably, without trying, you will do some of the most embarrassing things in front of students. Have you ever said a word or phrase that comes out wrong and you realize, too late, that it is not what you meant to say? Once I meant to say "bowl-shaped" and something else came out of my mouth. Not my finest teaching moment! It is up to you to decide how to handle these blunders. You can yell at your class and tell them it is not funny, or you can realize you made a mistake, have a good laugh together, and move on.

To add humor to your classroom, begin with the practice of laughing at yourself. Every good teacher should develop the gift of not taking himself or herself too seriously. You can use some self-deprecating humor with your students. However, don't overdo this. Lots of self put-downs might diminish your credibility and perceptions of your competence in the eyes of students or others in the school community. Students might even take on the habit of deprecating themselves, or worse, they might join in deprecating you because you sort of gave them permission!

If being funny doesn't come easily, you can include humor in a myriad of ways: puns, jokes, riddles, funny props, disguises, costumes, props, cartoons, funny articles or poems, clever anecdotes, or funny YouTube clips. (NEVER show any visual clip until you've viewed it on your own!)

Add humor (including cartoons) to your written study guides, class descriptions, review items, quizzes, or assignments. You can joke about, sing, dance, gesture, or act out important theories, processes, or concepts.

My good friend Neila Connors suggests giving flashcards with the words *Ha! Ha!* to a teacher who needs to learn how to laugh. The idea is that a teacher's aide or colleague sits in the class and holds up the *Ha! Ha!* cards when it's appropriate to laugh. If you're really deficient in the laughter category, you might try this to get you on the road to laughing. It probably won't take too many days of this tactic before you figure out when to laugh. By the way, Neila is the author of the must-read book *If You Don't Feed the Teachers They Eat the Students! Guide to Success for Administrators and Teachers* (2014).

Take Humor Seriously

While humor can help deflect tension, decrease classroom issues, help students learn, and bring the group together, it can also be harmful. Yes, be serious about incorporating humor for positive results, but also be serious about avoiding its pitfalls. If humor is used to divide or disparage, group togetherness is weakened instead of strengthened. Never use humor that mocks or denigrates anyone or any group. Don't single out a particular student. Don't use humor as a means of control. Never make fun of students in any way for their answers, ideas, beliefs, or behavior. Never describe or refer to a colleague with humor that denigrates that person (even subtly). The teacher's humor, used inappropriately, can escalate a situation with students because it can seem that you are putting a student down or taking sides. Humor can generate hostility. You set the tone for how humor is used in your classroom. Know that students are watching carefully.

I've just talked about students and sarcasm, but let's talk about teacher sarcasm. The topic is probably harder for teachers because, as adults, many of us are used to using sarcasm. It's so common that it doesn't seem harmful. It may be hard to even identify some comments as sarcastic. And you are probably mature enough to walk on the positive side of the fine line between positive and negative sarcasm, but few students are. And in truth, for most adults, it's hard to keep sarcasm nontoxic.

Even when subtle and not directed at a student, there is generally an insult somewhere in a sarcastic remark. Using sarcasm or laughing at it gives a signal from the teacher that it's okay to tease, nickname, or take jibes at people—if it gets a laugh. This kind of humor is not connective. Most experts and most young adolescents recognize sarcasm as a weapon. And we're trying so hard to stop the "passive" verbal bullying that is rampant in the school hallways and on social media! Use of sarcasm really gets in the way of our anti-bullying goals.

With middle school and high school students, you can use one-liner jokes and deeper levels of humor. You can even introduce students to sophisticated uses of humor such as irony and satire. But ban sarcasm from your repertoire.

For the most part, humor is a powerful tool in your efforts to embrace and bond with students, to help them feel comfortable, and to enliven learning experiences. But use humor maturely, with care and sensitivity to individual students. And as often as possible, link humor to your subject matter.

Use humor in ways that are comfortable for you. Be yourself. Don't try too hard. Don't wear any costume, tell any joke, use any prop, or read any story that makes you feel like a stand-up comedian impostor. Humor is real and genuine—not forced.

The Power of Knowing Them

Any teacher who chooses to work with young adolescents knows (or should find out really fast) what he or she is getting into. Young adolescents are engaging, irritating, immature, and sophisticated. They can play complicated musical instruments and elaborate digital games, figure out how to work any possible technological device, and conquer complex digital apps and programs. They can create museum-worthy art and write poetry that brings an audience to tears. They can work together in harmony to produce awesome creations. They can come up with shrewd observations and brilliant analyses. At the same time (and often on the same day), they can be sassy, clueless, uncooperative, forgetful, inept, and disinterested. Most of all, they are persistently changeable—intellectually, socially, physically, and emotionally. They have an overwhelming need to belong. And they have ever-present interests, issues, and influences that spill into everything inside and outside of school.

It makes an educator's head spin to keep up with who young adolescents are and what they need as a group—let alone try to know each individual student. But to do the best job we can to teach and nurture these students, *it's absolutely imperative that we get to know them.* And it's what they crave, even if they act as if they don't care.

At all times, try to remember what it was like to be in fifth, sixth, seventh, eighth, ninth, or tenth grade. Reclaim your best memories, worst memories, emotions, fears, questions, worries, successes, struggles, and joys. I won't go into all the details of the characteristics and needs of young adolescents here. Many of you know these well. If you need any refreshers on this, consult the list "Characteristics and Needs of Young Adolescents" in Appendix A.

Having those characteristics well in mind,

1. Make every effort to know some things about each individual student in your classroom, and, if possible, each student on your team. All students need personal attention, concern, and interest from the adults in their school lives.

2. Plunge into and stay engaged in the ongoing process of getting to know the fads and trends that engage the students. Young adolescents have their own culture, which is often reflective of the wider adult culture but with special twists. This culture is about the way they live and what they do—the norms, values, interests, language, and practices they share. A huge part of this culture

is outside the classroom, but it spills into the classroom in a thousand ways. Staying tuned into your students' world shows that you care enough about them to find out who they really are. This is challenging due to the likelihood of fads and trends changing in 24 hours. Certainly by the time this book gets into your hands, some things mentioned herein will be "so over"!

The Impact of Individual Connections

While you work at meaningful teaching, democratic classroom procedures, and relationships in general, go about the task of winning hearts one student at a time through individual personal relationships that are respectful and caring.

In middle schools and high schools, large numbers of students pass through each teacher's classroom. You don't have a lot of time to make contact with all those students. Here are a few ways to build a caring relationship with each student in short amounts of time:

- Pay attention to each student's individual passions, skills, worries, accomplishments, and challenges. Know something about their families. Keep notes on things you learn about each student. Keep track of their sporting events and other extracurricular activities. Notice their accomplishments in your class and other classes and outside of school. Yes, this means you might attend a basketball game that ends with a score of 7 to 12!

- Give students ways to tell you about themselves. Create surveys with questions about their lives, interests, the ways they learn best, and what they want you to know about them. Give them opportunities to write autobiographies or do photo essays showing what's important to them. Keep things they tell private, unless you have permission to share what they write or create.

- Make it a point to connect with each student on a personal-interest or personal-life subject at least once a week. Ask about something you know that student is "into." Comment on their activities such as sports, music, or arts. You can even make personal contact with each student every day by doing something as simple as smiling, saying "hello," or actively listening for a minute.

- Chat with students whenever you have a chance—in class, between classes, and in the hall. If time is too short for a chat, make sure high fives and handshakes abound. Always greet students by name. Always stand by the classroom door and acknowledge each student as he or she arrives and leaves.

- When you can, show up in the hallway and lunchroom and on the school grounds to make brief, friendly contact with individuals.

- Try to show up at events where your students are participating—games, debates, performances, parties, or dances. Your life is not complete until you attend a middle school dance recital.

- Let all students know that you're interested in them—what they like, what they know, what's happening for them. Try to get a sense of how things really are going for them and attempt to gauge the state of mind. Ask a student: "What's happening for you?" or "How's your week going?" or "Is this a good day for you?" or "Is anything bothering you?" or "What are you excited about?"

- Learn from the students. Ask individuals to explain to you the workings or details of something they are good at or are interested in.

- Acknowledge students when you see them outside of school around the community. Take the time to say a few words of greeting and meet family members or friends that might be present. (Freak them out when you see them; follow them around while pushing your shopping cart through Target.)

In many ways, the young adolescents in your classes are similar to young adolescents in other places—even in other countries. They often love the same movies, play the same video games, listen to the same kinds of music, are fascinated by the same things, try out the same fads and fashions, tell the same jokes, and laugh at the same things. Yet they so want to be unique. They want to be valued for their individual selves. Honor that! Affirm each one as an individual.

Connecting to the Adolescent Culture

Do you know what your students are up to? Do you know what they watch, listen to, digitally chat about, re-tweet, discuss outside of class, photograph, share on sites, are curious about, and do in their free time? Do you know what's in and what's out for them to wear, say, carry, eat, do, try, or like? Do you know about their gaming habits and what's hot in gaming? Do you know who and what they care about? Do you know who their role models are? If you've answered no to any of these—you have some catching up to do.

Here's a great activity for teachers: Come together as a team (or other group) and answer the above questions. Make a list of what you know about students' favorite shows, songs, celebrities, role models, technology, fashions, and games; their frequently-used phrases, jokes, slang, symbols, and abbreviations; and their consuming passions and interests.

For sure, your students have busy eyes, ears, and minds outside of their school subjects and activities. It's a given that today's young adolescents are interested in social networking. You can see with your own eyes that they live on their smartphones (sometimes ignoring the friend next to them while they "social" network). They constantly share (and over share) their lives with the help of various amazing apps, sites, and devices. They're interested in celebrities, fashion, cultural icons, entertainment, zombies, selfies, drones, virtual reality, music, dances, TV shows, movies, videos, and digital gizmos and apps that allow them to view or create all sorts of things. Many are deep into gaming. They communicate in their own language with slang, emojis, and texting abbreviations. The influences of pop culture, social media, and their peers are *mega-pervasive forces* in their lives.

And inherent in the interests, activities, and content of this youth culture, there's the ever-present fine line between what is appropriate or inappropriate for their developmental level. This is always in the adult consciousness.

If you want to understand your students and effectively teach them, you've got to know about this stuff. Really, you can't teach your students if you don't know them. And you can't know them if you don't learn about their world (weird, nauseating, or scary as some of it may seem). Furthermore, showing them that you are interested in their world and that you know *even something* about it is a downright dynamite way to connect with them. It shows you care. It shows you want to know them. It shows them you are not in outer space. Here are some thoughts about keeping up with the young adolescent world and making use of it in the classroom:

- Get to know their interests, fads, fashions, trends, and slang. To do this, you'll have to watch current popular TV shows, movies, and YouTube clips and hear some of the popular music. Read the lyrics; don't try to figure them out with your ears—it's nearly impossible. To know about their world means you'll have to listen hard, ask questions, and do some out-of-school research. This can take time, and what you learn about what they're saying and doing might be painful. But remember, young adolescents are always flabbergasted and honored when you make a reference to their current pop culture.

- Select appropriate references from pop culture to weave into classroom life and learning. To illustrate a key point in your teaching of a topic, refer to a line, name, event, or catchphrase from one of the latest games, songs, movies, or shows students love. Give a language lesson or written assignment for which they are only allowed to use emojis or text abbreviations. When the class is stumped for an answer to a serious learning-related question, interject a reference to a popular meme or song lyric. Although it might seem strange to hear this coming from you, the mood in the classroom will brighten.

- Ask students what their questions are—what they want to know about you and about the class. Ask them what they want *you* to know about them and their trends.

- Getting a class back on track might mean breaking into a current song that you know is a favorite. (Check those lyrics well before you start singing.) If you can't sing, that's even better!

- Show your enthusiasm about a great idea you're teaching or a difficult process students have just mastered (solving quadratic equations?) by breaking into a popular dance. Their jaws will drop! Insist it's an appropriate response to a big learning moment. (No dances with lewd movements, please!)

- Play appropriate popular music—particularly wordless music such as electronic dance music—while they do certain learning tasks.

- Give assignments that require students' use of critical thinking and critical reading skills to analyze TV shows, pop news, enticing Internet stories, or video clips. Give them a list of criteria for these evaluative tasks. Better yet, get them involved in developing the criteria. Use story lines, characters, or specific episodes for comparison projects.

- Find many ways to teach your students the evaluative skills they need daily to separate reality from unreality, to identify "false news," to describe what messages they are actually getting from media, and to make judgments about the messages and images from media and pop culture. This topic is tantamount to a whole new basic subject for their schooling. It's one of the very best things you can teach them for their real lives. They need to sift, create boundaries, make decisions, dismiss, and question constantly or they'll be swallowed up in a sea of unreality and misinformation. And to teach them to do this, you'll need to know something about the messages they're taking in!

- How many times have you overheard a student say something and you are not sure what it means or whether it is appropriate for school? Although you may act cool, students can tell that you are clueless. When you hear an unfamiliar phrase or word, ask your teammates or colleagues if they know the meaning. If all else fails, find a teenage neighbor or relative willing to spill the beans. (For some of us, "hip" is something we're getting replaced.)

- Be aware of changing trends in clothing—and this can happen very quickly. How many of you remember slap bracelets and girls with bangs so high they needed a building permit? The only fad that has stayed around for a long time is sagging pants, which, at last check, has been popular for 25 years now. That is the longest educational trend ever. I am not even sure phonics lasted that long! (Maybe if all teachers sagged, this trend would go away. I think students would be grossed out and pull up their pants.)

- Technology is part of the fiber of young adolescents. Integrate it frequently into their learning in real-life and meaningful ways. Require kids to complete a quiz by texting you the five answers, complete an outline by working together on Google Docs, or summarize a key idea in a tweet. However, also acknowledge the stresses their attachment to technology brings to their lives and brains—the constant pressure to be connected, the fear of being left out of social communications, the worries about what's being said about you on social media, and the addiction to games and apps. Knowing your students means embracing and addressing this part of their lives. Talk with them about all the benefits and consequences of "being connected." Learn what worries and frustrates them. And never feel bad about giving them breaks from technology!

- Invite students to teach you about their world. Do surveys to find out their favorite music, TV shows, activities, topics, video clips, news items, and celebrities. Ask who influences them. Ask what they think the adults in their lives should know. Ask them to show you how to work an app, do an online program, or play a video game. Let them develop a survey about their world for you to take to see if you know stuff they think you should "get."

- Be proactive in your school to involve the adults in learning about the youth culture that engulfs your students. Districts can burp up binders full of data. When was the last time your faculty or distract staff gathered data on, learned about, and discussed student social and emotional trends? When have you had an in-service day or series of seminars on how to use, combat, or deal with the influences of pop culture and technology use on students and their education?

When I'm Ruler of Education, every teacher will be issued a slang dictionary updated monthly. The kids can write it.

The Ever-Changing Slang

Even before their young adolescent years, students have a language of their own. The words and symbols they use, perhaps more than any other component of the youth culture, need particular attention. Teen language, including expressions, phrases, slang, emojis, symbols, acronyms, and abbreviations, has become a major concern for educators. There are ways that the new language of texting and other digital communications can be used in learning activities. But a huge amount of the popular teen culture communication needs to be off limits in any school setting.

This is so complicated. You may have never heard some of the very names, labels, or abbreviations directed at you by students. Keeping up with the language they use takes hyper vigilance and constant learning. The new slang comes and goes at lightning speed. There's an undercurrent of language on the school grounds, in the halls, mumbled under the breaths in classrooms, and communicated digitally during school hours.

Some utterances gain such widespread use in the culture that they become semi-acceptable. One such example is the use of the word *sucks* (at all ages—and even adults use it). Students often describe lessons or homework by saying they *suck*. Other common slang expressions find their way onto the school grounds even if they're banned—pejoratives such as *gay, queer, fag, stupid,* or the *N-word.* And there are hundreds of others, probably most of which we adults don't know what they are or mean.

When teachers hear these words, many have no response. Is it because we just don't hear it? Or are we consumed with so many other things that we just let it pass? Do we think, "I have to pick my battles, and this isn't one I'm picking"?

Here are some thoughts about how to address inappropriate slang. You can mix these in with or tack them on to your classroom or school policies about slang.

- Never pretend you did not hear a rude or derogatory comment or off-color remark. Address it immediately. No exceptions!

- Explain to students why certain words are not appropriate in the school setting. This is no different than our no-hats-worn-in-the-building or any other policy or school-wide rule. Well, actually it is way more serious than no hats!

- During the first week of school, make terminology the focus of a lesson. Have a thorough discussion of your expectations for acceptable language for formal and informal writing and speaking. Make sure students know that the discussion marks the beginning of everyone using appropriate language the rest of the year. Don't just drop the discussion after the first week of school. Reinforce this lesson consistently throughout the year.

- If you hear a new word and are unsure of its meaning, you can quickly find out by asking students or searching the Internet. Prepare yourself for a shock.

- Include new slang as a discussion topic at faculty meetings. Many staff members will be grateful to know that they can stop saying "thank you" when students call them something they do not understand.

- Be proactive about slang. No longer can we think: "I don't know if that word is appropriate or not." If we do not address some of these issues now, what words will be next?

Dealing with slang in all its forms is a monumental task. It involves making lots of decisions about what is acceptable and how to respond to what is not. This is too big a job for individual teachers to grapple with alone in their classrooms. It needs to be tackled by a whole faculty—even district-wide. Educators in a school or district must (and usually do) work out guidelines, boundaries, and policies. Many even have ever-changing lists of acceptable and unacceptable expressions with procedures for adult response and consequences for student misuse.

Whatever your school policy on slang, teachers, administrators, and even parents must teach students that certain words and other forms of expression are mean, can be offensive, and are not allowed in our hallways and classrooms.

Should we be frightened by the changes we are seeing, or should we embrace them? This is a difficult question because there are many possible answers. We could spend days talking about how we as educators must pick up the slack of society and teach everything from math to manners.

But one thing is clear: As teachers we play a key role in our society; in many cases, we are moral compasses for our students. Studies have shown that teachers, in addition to families and peers, have great influence on the beliefs and values of young adolescents (Weissbourd, 2003). Teachers certainly set examples. Our students watch and listen more carefully than we imagine to how we speak and how we respond to their use of language. Hmmm, thinking of us as role models can be frightening—I have seen what teachers can do in front of a karaoke machine or at a holiday party.

For Reflection and Action

1. Keep a record of how many students you can give attention or personal feedback in a day. It need not be public praise; any form of personal attention counts. See if you can reach all of your students in a week in some way.

2. Observe your students' developing senses of humor. Notice how you respond. Notice what impact this has on the style of humor you use with them. Can you recall ever resorting to sarcasm or other use of humor that, though not intentionally hurtful, was not the best decision?

3. List your methods for keeping current on youth culture—fads, trends, music, interests, fashions, games, etc.

4. What new things have you learned from your students in the past two weeks about their interests and their youth culture?

5. Are you finding your students fun to be with and your classes fun places to be? Do you laugh every day? If not, identify something new you'd like to try that you think could change this.

Source: *Managing the Madness: A Practical Guide to Understanding Young Adolescents and Classroom Management*
© Association for Middle Level Education
www.amle.org

CHAPTER 3

A Place Where They Want to Be

Mr. Berckemeyer, I can't see the board with Taylor's big head in the way!

Could it be time to give some long, hard scrutiny to your classroom—to the physical arrangement and the overall "look"? Do you need to redesign or discard outdated visuals? Could your students offer ideas on how to make some basic changes to the walls or even to the ceiling? Your classroom is a reflection of you and your students. Its ambiance, arrangement, contents, and function play major roles in classroom management. These things also make a big difference in your students' learning. Maybe it is time to give your classroom a makeover.

Review the total package of your classroom. Consider the furniture, equipment, supplies, arrangement of things, traffic flow patterns, and décor. The following survey (Figure 3-1) will help you think about this important aspect of students' lives (and your life) in relation to organization, workable procedures, student engagement, relationships, teacher morale, student morale, student comfort and safety, creating or avoiding potential problems, and overall classroom discipline.

Figure 3-1 *Evaluating Your Classroom*

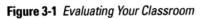

Check one or more answer(s) for each question.

1. The physical aspects of my classroom meet _____ .
   _____ my needs   _____ my students' needs
   _____ both my students' and my needs   _____ the needs of my students five or more years ago

2. I rearrange my room _____ .
   _____ frequently   _____ each season
   _____ once in a great while   _____ never or when forced

3. Students find my classroom _____ .
   _____ inviting   _____ uninviting   _____ filled with unique odors   _____ stimulating
   _____ creative   _____ boring   _____ comfortable   _____ distracting
   _____ I haven't asked or noticed what they think.

4. I display student work _____ .
   _____ always   _____ sometimes   _____ never
   _____ if I think it is worthy   _____ only during parent-teacher conference time

5. I rotate or replace the posters and other display materials _____ .
   _____ frequently   _____ after each project is completed
   _____ every quarter   _____ never   _____ when they get tattered or moldy

6. My classroom represents student interests _____ .
   _____ to the best of my knowledge   _____ not really
   _____ so much so that I took out a loan to pay for my purchases

7. The visual material around the room _____ .
   _____ teaches or reinforces learning concepts
   _____ is relevant to students and to what they are learning
   _____ has a purpose
   _____ is whatever I could find to stick up

8. As to the flow and arrangement of the classroom, _____ .
   _____ students are practically on top of each other
   _____ it always causes problems   _____ aisles are cluttered
   _____ everything is easy to find   _____ it allows for easy movement
   _____ there are places for group work and places for quiet.
   _____ what flow?

9. Materials and equipment _____ .
   _____ are easily accessible   _____ are hard to find or use   _____ are in messy piles
   _____ are always in their places   _____ are well organized   _____ are scarce or broken

10. Three new things I added to my classroom last month were

    _____ .

11. What I like best about the current classroom setup is

    _____ .

12. If I had unlimited resources, I would buy _____ for my classroom.

13. The two things I'd like to change first in my classroom are

    _____ .

Figure 3-1 *Evaluating Your Classroom, continued*

After completing the survey, answer these questions.

1. What are the strengths of my classroom environment?

2. What needs to change to increase workability, morale, or comfort?

3. Is the classroom meeting the needs of my students?

4. What items need to be added or removed?

5. Is there a better organizational process?

6. How can I improve traffic flow?

7. What are some new sources for good materials and resources to enhance the classroom?

8. How does the current setup encourage or discourage student interaction?

9. How does the current setup increase or minimize interpersonal clashes or discipline problems?

10. How can I involve students in making changes?

Source: *Managing the Madness: A Practical Guide to Understanding Young Adolescents and Classroom Management*
© Association for Middle Level Education   www.amle.org

Then, read this chapter and consider some ways you might improve, adapt, or reinvent your classroom environment. Keep in mind that the classroom environment needs to

- Contribute to everyone's overall physical and psychological safety, comfort, and morale.

- Offer intellectual stimulation.

- Provide a place where kids can learn and do their work.

- Enhance maximum learning and participation.

- Easily facilitate collaboration.

- Promote a sense of community.

- Help students take ownership of the classroom.

- Feel like home.

Seating Arrangements

Seating arrangements *do* have an impact on the learning process! They play a huge role in student participation and performance. Therefore, the arrangement of furniture is a key component in classroom management.

First of all, figure out how to keep your students close to you. It is all about proximity. The farther away they are, the longer the obstacle course of backpacks and notebooks on the floor to venture near to them. If students are far away from you, how do you know whether they are working on the assignment or doing something totally unrelated to the class—maybe texting a friend, cheating on the assignment, watching a video surreptitiously, viewing inappropriate websites on their phones, or sleeping? The farther away a student, the harder it is to make eye contact, observe, monitor, and interact.

Secondly, focus on what students will be able to see and hear from various locations. Every student must be able to hear you or any other speaker in the classroom wherever that speaker is located. Every student must be able to see whiteboards, projection screens, display boards, and demonstrations. A seating arrangement that blocks anyone's view or makes anyone squint or get out a telescope—or that leads anyone to ask for a hearing aid—is not a good one. Walk to the part of the room that is farthest from anything students need to see. If you can't see the board, screen, or display, neither can they!

Also, think about your teaching style, the ages and needs of the students, and the kinds of learning activities that will take place in your classroom. Of course, you'll also need to consider the space you have and the types of available furniture (desks, chairs with writing surfaces, large tables, small tables, "U" tables, etc.).

There are literally dozens of possibilities for room arrangements. Different kinds have different advantages and liabilities. In general, the old-fashioned rows are least desirable. You're far away from more than half of the students. Except for students in the front row, everyone is looking at the backs of heads rather than at other students. Circle arrangements foster whole-group dynamics. Tables are great for small group work; but if you want to bring students together, you have to move the tables. Some teachers love movable chairs (with writing surfaces) that can be arranged in many different group sizes and configurations. Decide what will work in your room. Don't be afraid to try different plans and certainly, don't hesitate to change seating for different activities.

Figure 3-2 *Seating in the Round*

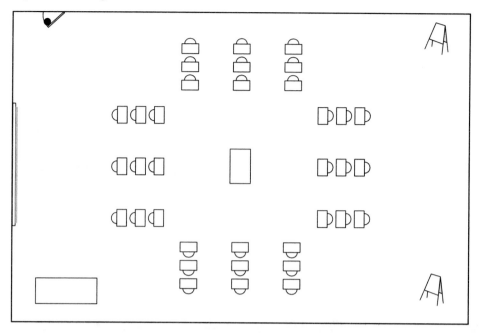

With seating, sometimes it is a good idea to start from scratch. Take everything out of the room, including the teacher shrine (better known as the teacher desk.) Then, making sure that no student's desk is more than three deep from you, fill in the room with your students' desks and other furniture. Figures 3.2 and 3.3 give a few diagrams of seating arrangements suggested by Rick Wormeli in *Day One and Beyond* (2003, p. 57).

Be creative and unique. Remember: if you and your students don't like it, you can change the arrangement in a couple of weeks or sooner, if urgent. Do some research about the current (and sometimes radical) changes in classroom layouts. Just as the adult workplace is changing, so classroom workspaces are changing. There is more attention paid to what is good for kids' spines and muscles. There are classrooms with desks where students can stand and work. In some places, chairs are being replaced with fitness balls, wobble chairs, floor cushions, or floor mats—all of which are good for spines, changing bodies, and comfort. In many classrooms, students no longer have personal desks. Personal materials are housed in crates or bins and furniture for seating is movable, flexible, and varied. Students use chairs, stools, tables, and other surfaces throughout the day as needed for the tasks they are doing. This encourages plenty of movement, which young adolescents need! If you're fortunate enough to have flexible, movable seating, survey the students to learn how they work best, then let them take the lead (with your collaboration) on the arrangement.

Figure 3-3 *Other Classroom Seating Arrangements*

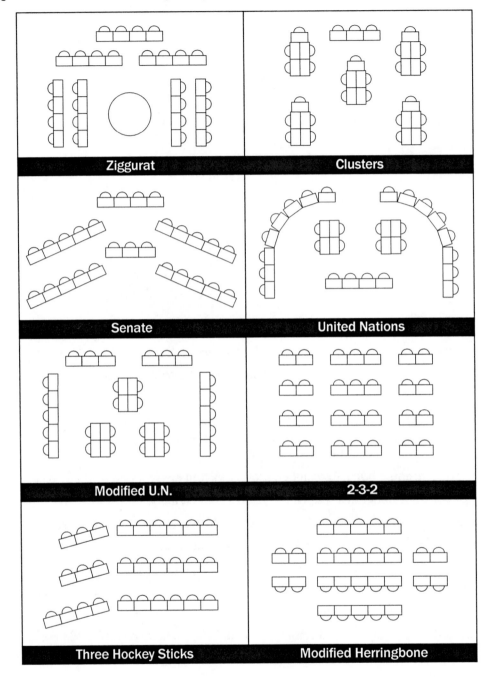

Clean and Tidy Should Be the Rule

When students walk into a trashed classroom with paper all over the floor, they will first be reminded of their own bedrooms. Although they might feel right at home, we need to aim for a hygienic and orderly environment that is more conducive to well-functioning brains. Keeping the room neat and clean is crucial; meeting this goal is a challenging task. The last few minutes before the releasing of the bulls (better known as the ringing of the bell for students to change classes) can be filled with chaos. You, of course, must do your part to tidy up your parts of the room. Also, set up regular procedures whereby students pick up clutter and wipe any gross things off surfaces before the end of the class period. Enlist students to help water plants, close windows, clean boards, and empty pencil sharpeners. In elementary school they loved to do these things—and many middle and high school students still do.

1. Find cheap plastic crates to hide all your papers and teaching materials.
2. Never let students leave until the room is clean.
3. Assign various housekeeping roles to students.
4. Invite students in for lunch to help with spring cleaning.
5. Ask parents to help after school with organization and cleaning projects.

Extreme Classroom Makeover

Although you may not have realized your classroom does have a direct connection to classroom behavior and management, when students walk into a classroom and get that first impression, they form important assumptions. They notice everything including how the room is arranged, how things sound, the brightness or dullness, the smells, the colors, the clutter, the order, the décor on the walls. If they see student work displayed, they'll know the teacher sees students' work as worthy and important. Also, students feel more ownership of the classroom when they see décor created by students or reflective of student interests and trends. The following thoughts and ideas may help with your makeover.

- Young adolescents know and care how up-to-date the posters and other materials displayed are. They get an immediate sense of how in tune or out of tune the teacher is. Yes, this means you may have to take down your N'Sync poster, that cute "hang in there" kitten poster, and other outdated possessions.

Discard the "READ" poster with yesterday's celebrities that your students don't know or care about. Be honest—some of the posters in your room might cause one to wonder if the featured celebrity could even read, was even interested in literacy, or is still alive.

- Some classics, of course, are worth keeping—for example, the inflatable T-Rex, the life-size cutout of you dressed in that unique spirit day outfit, or a strange saying or quotation that you use constantly. Such items deserve longevity and feature your personal character.

- One way to stay current with posters is to ask the manager of your local theater for posters of popular (and appropriate—not R-rated) movies. These are typically removed after the movie moves on, and often just tossed or recycled. The worst they can say is, "No," so why not ask? Be sure to tell the manager that you are a teacher. Build a relationship and he or she will start saving posters without your asking.

Remember, if you don't A.S.K, you have no chance to G.E.T.

- Drugstores and "big box" stores are good sources of free oversized boxes, posters, and signs. Visit the wallpaper store and scoop up books of wallpaper that are no longer in use. These provide tessellations and other geometric patterns for math. They also lend great color, texture, and design for book covers, display board backgrounds, or poster surfaces and that students can use to create their own visuals.

- Check home improvement, hardware, and paint stores periodically for mismatched or discontinued paints or for carpet squares or carpet pieces. You can wrap these carpet scraps around desks to muffle sounds or use the squares for padded floor seats. Confiscate those fun, colorful, out-of-date (or free) paint strips. Kids will love choosing color schemes to make the strips into name strips for their desks.

- Scour your local thrift shops and dollar stores for posters and other materials that have historic value. Believe it or not, adolescents still know Elvis and a few 60s and 70s, 80s, 90s, and turn-of-the-millennium pop icons. Use your judgment about which icons are suitable for featuring in your classroom. Students will even respond to some of the old original classic movie posters, especially if there has been a recent remake of the movie. You will be surprised at how some of the posters in your room can be conversation starters, forging connections between you and your students. The conversations help you learn about student's interests. And even students having trouble getting interested in science may join in on an anticipatory and surprisingly "heavy" lesson about the emotional nature of animals and whether King Kong had real feelings.

- Stock up on free or cheap plastic tubs—they help hide and store classroom items to keep your room neat.

- Consider asking your PTA or PTO to provide funds for a classroom makeover. Enlist parents or faculty friends to help you and your students create an improved learning environment. Be sure to lend your help when that colleague gets ready to give a makeover to her classroom or office.

Remember to get your principal's approval before you start a classroom renovation. It's a nice courtesy also to let the custodial staff know. They might just volunteer to pitch in. If students or parents are helping with any work, find out if it is necessary for them to sign any liability forms.

To expand your makeover into a team-wide or school-wide activity, run a contest. See what can happen with a little paint, creativity, and humor. Take into account guidelines (district policies) and stipulations (fire prevention regulations) to avoid having to dismantle a creation that covers an important piece of signage, is located too close to a vent, or poses a fire hazard.

Don't be afraid to rework the entire room or to bring something unique into the design. Once a teacher I knew found an old refrigerator door in a junkyard, cleaned it up, and mounted the door to a wall in his room. Students placed their favorite work on the door—an interesting and creative idea! I also met an amazing and creative teacher who used three discarded, cleaned-up toilets that he had mounted on a wheeled platform. He would wheel in the platform now and then. Students loved to take the seats while reading! (You gotta love young adolescents!) By the way, he had the empty water tanks—well cleaned and sanitized—filled with relevant, enticing reading materials. (The best part is: he was teaching a life skill!)

Student Input and Student Focus

Take time to create a room that incorporates student input and reflects their (appropriate-for-school) current interests. Young adolescents' tastes might change too quickly for us ever to keep up with the latest fads and trends, but they do love it when we attempt to stay current. Have you ever noticed the shock and surprise of your students when you make a reference to current pop culture as you are teaching? Students look at you as though you are from another planet. Although they probably know that teachers are human beings with human needs, they are floored by evidence that we shop at Target, eat at Chipotle, watch *The Walking Dead*, have seen *Deadpool*, watch reality TV, or listen to rock (or more shocking yet—to hip hop) music. We even sing loudly when driving in our cars (although it's possibly to Neil Diamond).

> Make that strange piece of furniture super glued to the floor with wax buildup an integral part of the classroom decor.

You can devote an area of the classroom to post bios of your students, samples of their achievements, and photos of them skiing, skateboarding, doing a craft, cheering at a game, attending a major sporting event, or just being a typical young adolescent.

Another way to engage students is by hanging such items as windsocks, wind chimes, or streamers near the heating and cooling system—they make for a great visual display. When air comes out of the vents, the fluttering kites, swinging windsocks, and sounding wind chimes might distract some students. And fire regulations must be considered of course. But if your students can handle the movement and still concentrate, they will be intrigued by the display.

Try painting the ceiling tiles: You can take them out of the ceiling and have students paint an entire ceiling with murals. Or, you can put subject matter related to your content area on the tiles. Such things as famous sayings, math equations, or science notations on the ceiling provide content to adolescents as they look up. For example, a science room ceiling might show the Periodic Table of Elements. Every social studies class should have a timeline on the ceiling. If painting the ceiling is not an option, you can still tack things on the ceiling or hang things from fishing wire or string.

Make sure that you follow your state's rules and remove all charts and other items as described in the rules for the state achievement tests. (I hate that I have to add that comment!)

If redesigning the whole room is a bit much, consider having a group of students design a section of your room and rotate the design group and the section of the room every couple of months. Think through when and how they will work most effectively and least invasively. High school teachers can ask the student government or a club to decorate the room. If this idea works for you, be sure to make a small donation to their club.

Creating a student-focused, safe place might cost a few dollars if it is to be vivid, creative, and interesting. However, students of all ages need and respect a place that is clean and visually exciting. Such a classroom sets a tone: it shows students you know who they are, what their interests are, and that you care about and respect them. They tend to behave better and learn more when they are respected and feel "known." When students are surveyed about teacher effectiveness or experience in a given class, they almost always comment on classroom environment.

One middle school teacher friend of mine fondly remembers a corner of her former classroom where students loved to relax and read. It featured a leather sofa and some tall trees planted in large pots. It was a welcoming, inviting refuge in an otherwise busy environment. This teacher also dimmed the lights to calm her students. (Classroom lights can raise the temperature of the classroom and don't always need to be on.) During a recent conversation with a group of young adolescents, an insightful seventh grader contributed this comment: "You can tell the personality of the teacher based on the teacher's classroom." Yes, you set the stage for learning by creating an environment that is truly student focused.

Those Dang Walls and Display Boards

Changing the boards and wall décor can be tiresome and challenging. So, why not let the students assume this responsibility? I always puzzled over how to make the classroom display boards engaging. I am not an artsy person—I struggle with drawing stick figures, and I am not naturally able to see how a huge square on the wall can be turned into a creative masterpiece. That is why I loved having willing and creative students. Offer students the opportunity to design meaningful boards. Let them take charge, be creative, and use their hidden talents to produce displays connected to the topic or unit under study. If you invite them to help, they can do amazing things to the room. Parents, too, like to help out, and this is one way they can stay involved in their kids' school lives. Note that the assistance of students and parents should not be viewed as a way of helping a too-busy, dull teacher but as an opportunity for students to investigate a topic, practice some skills, and lend their talents to creating learning experiences for all the students.

Ideas abound on the Internet for using display surfaces as tools for organization, classroom decoration, communication, student recognition, student sharing, review or reinforcement of learning, and even discipline or management reminders. Here are some basic suggestions to help you create an inspiring and student-friendly bulletin board:

- Students can add to the displays in ways that connect their personal interests to your subject. This empowers students and gives them some social interaction time as they work together.

- Design a backdrop for a wall or display board that has the following title and is otherwise left blank: "Student Show-Off Corner" (or "Gallery of Student Masterpieces"). Any student can choose to add something (appropriate) to the gallery!

- Ask local businesses to donate things such as oversized boxes and posters. Ask publishing companies for book jackets and cover proofs to display.

- Haunt bookstores for display materials they no longer want. These can be anything from stand-alone cardboard items to posters to items they had sitting on shelves or hanging from the ceiling.

- Have students generate a timeline for updating and keeping display boards current.

- Students can come in early, stay late, or work during lunchtime depending on your availability to supervise them.

- Snap photos of finished boards to help others generate ideas. This helps you remember what's been done. Also, you can share the ideas with others on Pinterest or other such sharing websites.

- Consider placing a "Giving Tree" outside your room with leaves that describe items you need. You might be surprised to see how parents will take the leaves of requests and make purchases for you or find objects or supplies in their garages, drawers, or attics. Be courageous—put a new interactive whiteboard on the giving tree. You never know, someone might show up with one! (I always put a new car on a list. Remember that if you don't A.S.K., you don't G.E.T.!)

In addition to the content and design of your bulletin boards, think of ways to use them to improve the order, function, and attractiveness of your classroom.

- Use old calendar pictures, newspaper pages, tests you've used in the past, wrapping paper, bags from retail stores, and other such random "patterned" items for display backgrounds.

- Always make sure you have a consistent spot on a wall or display board for regular, necessary features such as daily or weekly schedules, daily assignments and reminders, details of upcoming projects, upcoming birthdays, and special events.

- Keep a specific place for a daily post of the state content standard, essential question, or learning goal that will be a focus of the day's work. This lets them know what they will accomplish, master, or answer by the end of the class.

- Use a calendar posted somewhere in the room to list assignments for absent students.

- Designate a space to display accolades and awards for exceptional work and other deeds.

- Display your most essential policies and procedures (no more than five) on signs. When you find yourself repeatedly responding, "Read the directions," you can, instead, simply point to the sign.

- Use display boards for pre-teaching: display photos from magazines related to the upcoming unit; pose thought-provoking questions about the photos that will draw upon students' preconceptions and misconceptions; ask students to write what they would like to know about the topic.

- Use a board to display a list of words (or phrases, symbols, emojis, slang expressions, abbreviations, texting language) that cannot be used in formal writing or when giving written answers. Make it fun.

- Use the main board as a giant graphic organizer to show the relationships between the key concepts from an upcoming unit of study. You can fill it out as you give an overview the first day or "build" it with students as you progress through the unit.

- Post steps for processes students will use throughout the year—for example: rules for working in the lab, what to do when running into a reading comprehension obstacle, how to solve a particular type of problem, or how to structure an essay.

- Write vocabulary words from the chapter on one wall or board (call this your "word wall") and put a visual image with each word. If there are comparative terms (*exothermic, endothermic*), color code the words linked to *exothermic* with one color and those linked to *endothermic* another color.

- Use a display area for a resource that can extend learning on a particular topic. Display captivating photographs and articles containing content you won't have time to cover when teaching the unit. This gives students extra, engaging information to expand what they've learned.

- Capture student attention and further their thinking with content-related cartoons.

- Find an image of a real-life person, fictitious character, or comic book character that might appeal to students. Scan the image and project it onto a mural; invite students to color it. They can add words or phrases that indicate what they have in common with the character or what questions they'd like to ask the character.

- Form a border around the room with book covers.

- Don't forget music! Sometimes this gets forgotten beyond the elementary classroom or the official music class. Music enhances language, expression, memory, brain development, and enjoyment of the environment! Find ways to introduce students to a variety of kinds of music (yes, classical and jazz too). Open and close the class with music; use music to teach and reinforce concepts; calm students with music before a test; and use music for smooth transitions between activities.

As you revisit, reconsider, and perhaps restructure or rehab your classroom environment, be sure to give it your personal touch. You are one of the citizens of the classroom. Just as it should reflect your students, it should reflect you!

We all know that content, curriculum, instruction, assessment, and other such academic matters are important. So are the practical and personal matters that enable sound teaching and learning. For proven best practices and frontline advice on managing the physical and emotional aspects of your environment, I recommend that you read Rick Wormeli's fine book, *Day One & Beyond* (2003).

For Reflection and Action

1. What are the main functions you want your display walls and boards to perform? How successfully have they served these functions?

2. What would you like to do to improve the content and usefulness of your displays while making them student-centered and engaging?

3. Describe some examples you have seen of ways the classroom environment contributes to or detracts from effective classroom management.

4. Describe some examples you have seen of ways the physical environment affects student success.

5. In what ways is your classroom a reflection of your teaching style?

6. How have you increased student voice and choice through your classroom setting?

7. Describe one significant change you have made in your classroom's physical environment and ways it has affected your classroom management.

Source: *Managing the Madness: A Practical Guide to Understanding Young Adolescents and Classroom Management*
© Association for Middle Level Education   www.amle.org

Move Engagement, Less Madness

*Mr. Berckemeyer, I need to walk around the room at least ten times an hour.
It helps me focus.*

One thing is for sure in the young adolescent years: *change.* It's exciting. It's baffling. It's weird. It's magical. It's unpredictable. It's scary. And these words describe *your* feelings. Imagine what it's like for the kids! Much of the behavior of young adolescents is linked to their rapid and erratic physical, emotional, and cognitive development. And thus the life of any teacher in a middle school or high school will not lack for moments of surprise, high drama, humor, and frustration.

As young adolescents go through changes highly powered by hormones, they experience such new habits and impulses as increased twitching, a constant need for movement, and rapid mood swings. They can go from having vast amounts of energy at their desks (or OUT of their desks) to sleeping on the floor in a matter of minutes. You can assign a silent writing, reading, or research activity and then watch a young adolescent male make the most unique facial expressions while his arm is swinging around in the air. Seemingly unable to control his body movements, he lets out a gigantic, loud sigh that could cause a tsunami halfway across the world. If you summon the courage to ask, "Are you okay?" he'll look at you and say, "WHAT?" He is totally clueless that he has released an earth-shaking amount of energy in just a few seconds.

Yes, they tap, click, pat, shuffle, hum, whisper, make animal noises, burp, pass gas, and make faces—usually all within the first two minutes of class. They giggle, gasp, hide under hair or hoodies, guffaw, hold their noses, and react to one another in all sorts of ways from goading to groaning to applauding. Their rapidly changing bodies leave them feeling awkward and worried. Their rapidly growing brains do not make the same connections as mature adult brains, so they have ways of thinking all their own. They want to be liked by their teachers but can't resist testing them. With their frontal lobes not yet matured, their decision making, behavior choices, and impulse control are all far from mature. They tend to live in the moment, think the world revolves around them, obsess over the importance and approval of their peers, want to be seen as grown up but revert to childish behaviors when embarrassed or stressed, alternate between lofty self-views and poor self-esteem, operate on feelings rather than reason, and are distracted by a thousand social, emotional, and physical needs. This is all very pronounced in the middle level years, but extends far into high school.

Even more complicated for young adolescents and the adults in their lives is this: no two of them are changing in exactly the same way or on the same timetable. I stopped by a café in a town where I was working last week to grab coffee and a bagel. Within a few minutes I realized that I was the lone adult among 28 young adolescents. My sleep-deprived brain slowly figured out that this was the before-school gathering place for students headed to the middle school around the corner. A boy who looked about eight sat next to a mustached boy who could have been a forward for an NBA team. Some of the girls looked 20; others were obviously prepubescent. Voices that filled the small room varied from deep and booming to high and squeaky. Their fashions ranged from haute couture (lots of makeup with these) to pajamas. Every one of them held and pecked at a digital device. I heard sounds of blow-em-up video games mixed in with serious phone discussions about relationships.

In about half an hour, they would all be clamoring into classrooms and—voila! Not only would a group of teachers have the job of managing them but would be expected to teach them, as well. And those two things (managing and teaching) are the most dynamic pair of endeavors a teacher would ever want to attempt! And hurrah for me! I was headed to that very school to speak to their teachers about classroom management!

Okay, I'm going to stop right here and summarize one of the primary messages of my talk with their teachers. It also happens to be the main point of this chapter. I'll put it to you straight and simply: *A classroom with dynamite, engaging learning activities is a classroom with management success.* **Period!**

If you understand who your students are developmentally, know what they need, and provide learning experiences that resonate and captivate, you'll have a classroom where students are *way less likely* to get into the usual management difficulties. But you have to *get* the realities of their changes and needs! And you have to know what those realities mean for the classroom and adapt everything you do and say to embrace them!

Due to such factors as more rigorous content, high-stakes testing, and new standards, attention to students' development has diminished in many schools. But great educators of young adolescents never forget that you need both content expertise and understanding of development. Regularly review the developmental characteristics and phases of your students. See the list "Characteristics and Needs of Young Adolescents" in Appendix A.

The Engaging Environment

The last chapter gave you ideas for the physical attributes of a classroom for young adolescents. But, a learning environment is far more complex than furniture arrangements and wall décor.

Armed with understanding about the students' developmental characteristics, needs, and changes, we can go beyond the physical classroom arrangements to focus on the elements that create an inviting, effective climate where they can flourish academically. This environment is positive with upbeat energy. It bustles with intellectual activity, physical activity, collaboration, questions, creativity, curiosity, laughter, and vigorous instruction. It's fueled by cooperative learning as well as personalized learning. It is free from threats to physical or emotional safety and from other blocks to learning. Engaging experiences are available to and geared to all students. There is a central understanding that everyone is valued and that everyone can succeed. And it's dynamic! Fun, humor, celebration, and accomplishment abound.

Everything you do and say affects your students' learning. This includes your body language, tone of voice, and even the slightest nuances of attitude or prejudice. I know this may be scary, but it's true!

And guess what? This environment begins (and continues) with YOU! You are its number one purveyor. ALL the messages about learning emanate from you. Yes, the room is inviting, senses are stimulated, the visuals promote interesting ideas, and the furniture is arranged for maximum learning and good management, but the tone of the décor means little without the human being who carries the tone forward. All your actions make a difference in how they see themselves as students and how they perform as students. Young adolescents, in particular, miss nothing. They are always, always watching and listening, even though they are very, very good at acting as if you don't exist. So check to see that your hair looks good and your pants are zipped, and step onto the runway with full awareness of the spotlight.

Show students you believe in them and their abilities. Show them you believe they can overcome difficulties, tangle with hard stuff, and master tough concepts. Expect them to succeed, but make it clear that it is safe to struggle and question. Make sure every single student knows you are his or her advocate. Model all the learning attributes you want them to acquire:

- Creativity, collaboration, and open-mindedness.

- Responding to setbacks, failures, and mistakes by trying again.

- Setting and articulating goals and evaluating whether you reached them.

- Consistency and follow-through.

- Explaining your thinking or how you solved a problem.

- Persistence, risk taking, and trying new things.

- Passion, energy, and love of learning. Let them see your curiosity and where it takes you. Let them see your excitement about ideas, processes, or discoveries. Show them that you like your job and that you like being with them. Spread positive energy, hope, and delight.

- Reflection. Openly reflect on your lessons and techniques.

- Positive, useful feedback. Ask them for feedback about you—about your lessons, strategies, attitudes, or communications with them.

- Flexibility. Let them see you change course when needed, change up a teaching approach, or incorporate unexpected things that come along.

- A good sense of humor. Laugh a lot.

- Pride in the students. Let them see your thrill over their accomplishments, persistence, and hard work.

- Belief. Perhaps most important of all: never give up on a student. Be sure every student knows you would not give up on him or her or anyone else in the class!

Meeting Student Needs

Students are far more likely to succeed academically when they are engaged in the learning. The engaging environment described at the beginning of this chapter is grounded in the needs of young adolescent students. This is the only path to assuring that the students will be engaged. And engaged students are far more likely to succeed academically. What follows are ideas for connecting learning experiences to some critical needs of young adolescent students.

The Need to Feel Normal

Even more important than you understanding what's going on with your students is their need to figure it out themselves. Don't take it for granted that they've had a lot of preparation or explanation for what is happening to their bodies—including their brains, emotions, and hormones. Let them know that these vast changes are entirely normal. They so badly want to feel normal! Help them understand that part of this normal is that everyone's pace and specifics of change are different. Understanding this can lead to less anxiety and greater acceptance of growth variations, decrease fears about what is and isn't happening, and result in fewer judgments about other students' changes (or lack of changes).

You can help young adolescents weather the tumultuous middle school and early high school years. They can feel calmed and supported by your *complete acceptance* of the erratic changes and your excitement about the significance of their changes. Here are a few ways to turn their growth experiences into learning experiences while helping them feel comfortable with and proud of the changes:

- At the beginning of the year, take individual photos of your students next to a particular poster or other visual. Halfway through the year and again at the end of the year, take photos in that same spot with the poster in the same place. Students will be able to see how they have grown and changed in just a few months.

- Each student can take a string measurement early in the year. Extend a string from beneath one shoe to the top of the head. Cut the string, roll it up, and label it with the student's name. Return the strings to students at the end of the year. I guarantee you will have at least one student say, "Ms. Altimiaro, this is not my string." Meanwhile the teacher is thinking, "Is your name on the string? Then it is yours. Does he think I came in and changed the names?" Students will be surprised at how the string now only reaches their shoulders or noses. If a student's string still extends from head to foot, make assurances that different growth timelines are normal. I thought it was strange once when a student's string was bigger at the end of the year than he was. Maybe he actually did shrink that year.

- Middle grades students like to trace their bodies on mural paper early in the year and again at the end of the year to show how much they've changed. Just be vigilant about any drawing of body parts they might decide to add on the life-size body drawings!

- Students can also make ink prints of their hands and feet (as was done when they were born). Post the handprints and footprints in the hallway along with such a label as "Walking Towards Our Future" or "Where are We Headed?" They could also write poems or thoughts about where their hands and feet might take them that year. Re-do this at the end of the year and compare the prints.

- At the beginning of the year, line up students in order by their birthdays. Take a picture. Re-take this mid-year and at the end of the year. Notice differences in height, arm length, hair, and facial features.

The Needs for Safety and Security

In order to focus their brains, students need to feel safe and secure. Challenging, engaging activities stimulate the brain, but learning is thwarted when a threat is perceived. Discomfort and fear inhibit attending to, processing, and remembering information (Caine & Caine, 2015, pp. 33-53).

In addition to obvious needs for physical safety, safety in the classroom involves emotional matters (see Chapters 2, 5, and 6). Students need:

- Belief in the teacher's care and commitment to each student.

- Predictability of routines (knowing the rules of the game).

- Clarity of behavioral expectations and consequences.

- Assurance that the teacher will hold students to stated procedures.

- Evidence that the teacher will not allow bullying (even "silent" bullying) or other forms of disrespect.

- Experience of positive teacher-student and student-student relationships.

- Participation in specific strategies to help every student feel a sense of belonging.

Another part of security in the classroom is academic safety. Students need to:

- Know the routines, procedures, and expectations surrounding learning experiences.

- See that the teacher knows where the work of the day is headed and communicates what they'll need to do to succeed.

- Be clear about the criteria for success, how their progress will be tracked, and how their work will be evaluated.

- Know that it's okay to question, fail, struggle, and succeed.

- Have assurance that help will be available when they're lost or confused.

- Feel confident that their questions, answers, or products will never be belittled.

- Believe that their hard work will be noticed and affirmed.

The Need to Move

Do you know that at the onset of puberty the lower part of young adolescents' spines fuse together, making it uncomfortable to sit for long periods? Could this be why they constantly get up to move around the room? Could this explain why the pencil is never sharpened enough or why the piece of paper needs to be placed in the trashcan (or shot across the room to the trash basket) during the most important part of your lesson? Could this be why some of the boys never, ever sit up straight but always have their legs four feet into the aisle—turning their desk spaces into lounge chairs? Could this be why they rock in their chairs while you feel the need to chant, "Four on the floor"? (Meanwhile several students are thinking, "It is really six on the floor if you count *my* legs.")

It is a simple fact: adolescents will move, with or without permission. Our goal should be to accommodate this need by getting them to move with purpose. When I taught sixth grade, I had students who would just walk around for no reason. When I asked, "Do you need something?" or "Can I help you?" they would just look at me and say, "No I am fine, I am just walking around." Invariably standing in front of me as I was trying to teach, these students were totally oblivious. That is when I began the habit of pulling large clumps of hair from my head! I had failed to realize that I needed to give them opportunities and purposes for moving around.

When kids start fidgeting, it's a normal physiological sign that their brains are going to sleep. Catch the signals before the fidgeting starts. Students need a brain break about every 20 to 30 minutes. Build some sort of movement or change of position into every learning experience as well as before, after, and between learning tasks. This keeps their brains awake and engages them with the concepts and processes. Here are a few ideas to get them moving:

- Dry erase boards can be a teacher's best friend. Place one under every student's desk. When you ask a question, students can write their answers on the boards. If they don't know the answer, they can draw a question mark. When they are done, they use both hands to hold the boards up as high as they can reach. This forces them to stretch and sit up straight. In addition to engaging academically, they are physically active in a way that's good for their muscles, blood flow, and air intake.

- Tell students you will make a statement or give a possible answer to a question. They must listen carefully and decide if they support the statement or answer. If so, they are to stand up next to the desk to show their assent. This keeps their brains attentive to the statements or questions and gets their bodies moving.

- Ask a question and give two possible answers. Students clap twice if the answer is A and three times if it is B. Again, a simple movement can help encourage participation.

- Create a catchphrase or statement relevant to your lesson. Tell students that when you use it, they are to respond with some appropriate gesture, noise, or chant. For example, whenever I said the phrase "mad scientist" in a diagram-accompanied lesson on science fiction, the students could shout,

"BOO-HA-HA." Yes, it seems strange. But it was great for finding out if students were attending to the information. Saying "mad scientist" randomly, I always hoped my students were paying attention. However, sometimes the only response I got was the hissing noise from the outdated heating unit in the corner. Then suddenly a student would snap out of her educational coma and do the "BOO-HA-HA," causing others to return to this planet and follow suit. Eventually, the class would perk up and start paying attention.

- The next time you realize that students have been sitting for more than 20 minutes for some learning activity, come up with something that forces them to move. They need the change of pace, and it just might decrease the number of random walkabouts during the most important part of a lesson. For example, on a particular signal, students can jump out of their seats and move two seats to the right to continue their work. Or they can do ten seat squats (stand up, bend knees until bottom touches seat).

- Build a repertoire of one- to three-minute brain-break activities. Include such things as stretches; arm, hand, or foot movements; gentle massage or pressure to muscles; body shaking; dancing; drumming; tapping; or chair aerobics.

- Work a trash can quiz into the teaching repertoire once in a while. It's a lot like the old bucket and ping pong ball game on Bozo Circus (I know this is a pretty old reference. You young teachers may have to look it up on the Web. Beer pong might be a more modern example.) Here's how it works: You place five buckets at various distances from where the participating student stands. The bucket that's farthest away holds the hardest question and is worth the most points; the closest basket holds the least difficult question and is worth the fewest points. The student chooses the difficulty of the question and tosses the ball toward a basket. This gets kids up and moving while they have a good review for an upcoming test.

- Use a current dance move to start class. Similar to the problem-of-the-day concept, you can have a dance of the day. Use this dance when transitioning students from activity to activity. They get to dance and move together. (Avoid the word *movement* as it might get more guffaws than you want to deal with.)

- Explore the book, *Brain Gym: Simple Activities for Whole Brain Learning* or the Brain Gym website: www.braingym.org.

The Need for Active Learning

One of the things we know about the adolescent brain is that abstract thought processes are not well developed until ages 18 to 20. Thus, students need concrete experiences to find meaning in symbols and abstractions. If information does not have meaning, they're unlikely to pay attention to it!

Active learning is not the same as physical movement, though it may involve moving. It is learning by being *involved* in an experience (as opposed to learning by watching or listening). There is another, critical part to active learning: The student is not just *doing* something, but is *thinking* about what he or she is doing. The student has a concrete (involved, hands-on) experience *and* then reflects on such questions as: "What happened?" "What works?" "What doesn't work?" "What does it mean?" and "Why?" Make active learning endeavors the norm in your classroom. Attach learning concepts, processes, and review to such concrete learning tools, practices, and products as:

recordings	murals	games
posters	painting	cartoons
parades	sculptures	learning centers
dramatizations	photographs	simulations
map-making	media presentations	designs
timelines	rubrics	demonstrations
diagrams	flow charts	labs
charts	symbol cards	interpretative dances
graphs	montages	rhythmic patterns
graphic organizers	scrapbooks	original songs or raps
collages	visual webs	role playing
animation	dances	collections
exhibits	impersonations	use of any equipment or tools
videos	pantomimes	
models (physical, digital, mental)	reenactments	use of any art form
	theatrics	use of interactive technology
audio recordings	storytelling	

The Need for Variety

Young adolescent learners need variety. Their teachers do, too. (Rigor mortis can easily set into the adult in the room if things are too sedentary, ordinary, or repetitive.) Yes, certain processes do need repetition. But even so, the brain benefits from repeating processes in new ways with different content and from repeating content in new ways with different processes.

So switch up activities. Approach a concept many times, changing the learning model, pace, place, materials, topics, tools, applications, content, and questions. Include many different strategies in your lesson plans: groups, pair learning, students teaching students, inquiry, projects, interviews, experiments, problem solving, summarizations, simulations, comparisons, performances, explanations, technology use, and retellings. Include ideas and information from multiple sources in multiple formats. All of these approaches give chances to differentiate learning for the many different needs, levels, and learning styles of your students.

The Needs for Familiarity and Novelty

We teachers know this principle: it's easier to learn something if we can link it to something we already know. Not only is it easier to learn, but also the connection to prior knowledge brings deeper understanding to concepts. We often tell students to think about or write down what they already know about a topic. It's a good starting point for expanding knowledge on the topic. This relaxes students and takes away some of the fear of the unknown. It immediately de-stresses the brain and sets it churning because there's already some familiarity with the concepts.

At the same time, the brain craves novelty. Teens and pre-teens are particularly susceptible to novelty. Something new and surprising really excites the brain and grabs its attention. In fact, if there isn't something surprising, the brain will wander somewhere else. Enhance handouts, assignments, review exercises, or tests with cartoons or other drawings to help stimulate thinking or illustrate key points. Grab attention with items and experiences that stimulate all the senses. Change routines, locations, approaches, and sometimes schedules. Bring in new materials, visitors, and accessories.

Keep students engaged with a good balance of familiarity and surprise. All of the ideas in this chapter can help you with this balance.

The Need to Socialize

It's one of the 12 brain/mind learning principles synthesized from research related to the brain and learning: "The brain/mind is social" (Caine & Caine, 2015, p. 54). The brain learns better in concert with other brains. "All students have the capacity to comprehend more effectively when their needs for social interactions and relationship are engaged and honored" (Caine & Caine, 2014, p. 4). Students need many chances to express their ideas and opinions, work and learn with others, conference with peers, get and give feedback, resolve conflicts together, and converse in a variety of ways. Find ways for students to create, discuss, question, decide, ponder, research, solve, experiment, produce, evaluate, and reflect in pairs and groups. Given this brain need, is it any wonder that young adolescents love social media and constant digital connection?

Collaborative, or social, learning has wonderful benefits. Groups or teams working together remember and understand concepts longer and think at higher levels than students working individually. Students feel a sense of belonging, and have chances to develop new and better peer relationships. They get face-to-face interaction, experience positive interdependence, and increase social skills. Together, they learn to process ideas and get the satisfaction of accomplishing mutual goals. Individually, students feel responsible, dependable, needed, and accepted.

Make sure that cooperative learning has a major role in your classroom. Use cooperative strategies such as think-pair-share, interviews, group research or team investigations, jigsaw, three-minute review, quiz-quiz, sixteen-word summary, and numbered heads together. You can find details of these and other strategies online. I recommend that you investigate Dr. Spencer Kagan's structures for cooperative learning in his many publications on the topic (1992, 1995, 1997, 2013, 2015). Also, find time to review Rick Wormeli's book *Differentiation: From Planning to Practice* (2007) for fantastic details on flexible grouping to meet the needs of a wide range of learners within the same classroom.

Some Advice on Group Work

Grouping students— Putting students into groups can be a two-minute ordeal or may cause friction for an entire grading period. Your day with young adolescents is not complete unless you hear "Is this the same group as last week?" or "What group am I in again?" or my personal favorite, "I hate my group!"

Even if you plan well, you'll probably hear some of the above comments. Hopefully, with a lot of group work, students will calm down and get used to the process. Speaking of planning—most collaborative learning experts recommend against two things: (1) letting students group themselves and (2) selecting groups randomly. It might be fun now and then to group students by passing out playing cards on all the desks and having them find group members with the same card suit. But most of the time, groups should be thoughtfully targeted and planned. And they should be heterogeneous—a diverse mixture of abilities, academic strengths and weaknesses, interests, learning styles, genders, personalities, and social groups. The optimal size for a group is from two to six students. (Many experts say a group of four is optimal.) A group may stay together for a while to complete a particular process, but mix up the groups often so students get to know and work with diverse and varied combinations. Don't change groups in the middle of a task.

Getting ready for group work—Before students work in groups, make sure they are well initiated to the protocols and roles for group work. Even if students have worked in groups other years or in other classes, make your expectations clear. Get students involved in deciding the protocols. (See the "Working in Groups" section on the next page.) Take time to help students learn skills for resolving conflicts that will arise during group work.

Always give a purpose and clear direction for each specific group work time. Students should know what the group task is (goal or goals), what the outcome is to be (product, question answered, etc.), what is expected of the group and of individuals, how the work will be graded, and how much time they'll have. Explain this well. Repeat it. Write it down where it can be reviewed. Show the task and expectations in several places—on the board, on each table where a group will work, or in a handout for each student. When you're asked, "What are we supposed to do?" you can point to the sheet or list; students will learn to track their own way through the task.

Solidify the understanding of the directions this way: Ask a student from one group to repeat the first step (or direction) of what they are to do. Have a student from another group give the next step. Continue this until all directions are reviewed.

Identifying group roles—Before starting group work, set up roles for specific jobs (facilitator, recorder, timekeeper, summarizer, presenter, researcher, materials manager, data collector, etc.). You can assign the roles for each group, or students can determine roles when they get into their groups. Be sure that students know the expectations for each role; write these on cards that they can keep with them in the group.

Moving students in and out of groups— Display group members' names on the board or wall. Even better, write them on large pieces of paper and post them around the room; this gives students a reason to walk around and find their groups. Yes, it will be loud and even a little crazy. Have students gather all necessary materials and stand up before they move to another part of the room for group work. This will avoid their making constant trips back to their original desks.

Before students move in or out of groups, give specific directions as to where they'll be going and what they'll be doing when they get there. Make a visual check to see if everyone is ready. Then give the cue to move to groups. Set a time limit and make it fun. For example, tell students they have 40 seconds to get to their new locations. Do an exaggerated countdown. You can be "over the top" to get them moving more quickly. It might resemble the running of the bulls in Pamplona, Spain, but it is effective.

Sometimes, use music for transition time. Students learn the music that is played during specific activities, and their response to the music becomes automatic. Use different styles of music for different transitions. This is a nice way to broaden their acquaintance with musical genres and artists.

Working in groups—Set protocols for how students are to work and relate in groups. This way, they will know how to interact when they get together. Students can contribute to the ideas for group-work rules. Agree ahead of time on such behaviors as:

1. Be prepared. Bring your materials and any information or work that you are supposed to contribute.

2. Be responsible for your individual roles and for accomplishing the group task and goals. Don't stray from the task. Do your fair share of the group's work task.

3. Be an active participant. Be willing to give your ideas. Contribute interesting, quality comments. Respond to other people's comments. Build on their ideas.

4. Work with quiet, normal voices. Watch out for escalating noise!

5. Listen politely to others' ideas and opinions. Wait for the person speaking to finish before you speak.

6. Always support your group's work. Be respectful and encouraging. Help to make sure everyone understands and everyone succeeds.

7. Don't "check out" or wander away. Never indulge in distractions such as side conversations, texting, or bothering other groups.

8. Help to clean up.

Reflecting and evaluating—Always provide a way for group members to review and evaluate their work together. They can use a set of questions, a reflection guide, or a rubric. The group should reflect on the process they followed, the accomplishment of the group goal, and any difficulties that arose. Together, members can identify strengths and needs of the group process and set goals for future work. Also offer opportunities and strategies for individuals to reflect on their contributions to the group work.

Supporting the groups—What do you do while students are in groups? This is simple: ROAM. Your roaming will prevent their roaming (physical or mental). Continuously move around the room. This puts you in the midst of the groups—ready to answer questions, monitor their work, and handle issues that arise. Roadblocks to group work change daily and include students being off task, a group member feeling lost or confused, students wandering around the room bothering other groups, and—the most common—one group that is not even close to being done when all other groups have finished. Constantly check the progress of the groups, moving troubled groups closer to you if needed. Do not hesitate to remove students who are major distractions to their groups.

Allowing for off-topic socializing—Definitely realize that when young adolescents are in a group, they will socialize. It is part of who they are; they crave interaction with their peers. Their need to laugh, debate, and argue in groups helps students grapple with social norms and build social skills. This is a key part of their development. If you have special concerns about a student, place him or her facing you or with their back to you so they don't know when you are there. Friends can be placed back to back. But expect and allow for a certain amount of socializing that is a bit off topic. When, oh when, has a group of educators ever gotten together—even to accomplish some major, serious task—and not spent some time socializing? If you can name one time, I'll have to question your veracity.

The Need for Competence

Every student wants to feel capable and successful at taking on learning challenges. Young adolescents can fool you. They can look as if they don't want to learn, show apathy toward anything that happens in school, feign indifference to the most scintillating classroom activities, and—in particular—let you know that they already know everything anyway. They are masters of disinterest. Some of them even pretend to be dumb to gain approval from their friends (boys often do this) or to keep from threatening other students (girls often do this). But you are not fooled. You know that they want to be competent and that they want you to believe they can be. Furthermore, the kids who experience academic success and feel good about themselves as students are likely to stir up few management problems.

> When I'm Ruler of Education, I'll issue this edict: students will have time to socialize (without the teacher shushing them or redirecting them) in every class or group period!

All of our students deserve top-notch instruction that is highly interesting, challenging, and targeted to individual needs. Let students know you take them seriously as students and believe firmly that each one of them can accomplish academic goals. There isn't room in this book for a treatise on excellent teaching, but here are a few things to keep in mind to meet the students' needs for competence:

- Prize academic rigor and vigor.

- Set clear academic goals and help students meet them. Help them learn to set their own.

- Make sure students know what they have to do to meet the goals.

- Give students lots of opportunities to think critically (analyze, evaluate, use evidence and reasoning to support thinking, interpret information, solve complex problems, make reasoned decisions).

- Connect topics, lessons, and tasks to real-world situations.

- Balance the amount of time you talk with the amount of time that students talk. (In fact, students should talk more than you talk. By talk, I mean, use their voices in many ways to participate in learning situations.)

- Ask quality questions (questions that demand higher-level cognition). Teach students to ask quality questions. Let students see that questions are more important than answers.

- Make, "So what?" a common question in your classroom. With any concept students learn or explore, get them thinking about why it makes a difference, what its wide-reaching benefits or consequences are, and why it's good to know this. The question "So what?" pushes reflection and deeper thinking.

- Give students challenging work (things that promote higher-level thinking). One of the brain/mind learning principles is that "complex learning is enhanced by challenge" (Caine & Caine, 2015, p. 35). Every time you push your brain, it gets a little smarter. Let students know that frustration is normal and that they'll be pleased with what happens when they push their brains beyond what they think is possible.

- When challenging students, be ready to offer scaffolding techniques (where needed) to increase their chances of success.

- Give students time to think. Let them sit and wait with an idea. Give them time to grapple with challenging questions, texts, problems, concepts, and tasks. The brain needs time to engage with challenging ideas.

- See that every student can identify his or her academic strengths and can revel in noticing them at work!

- Give regular recognition to effort, persistence, accomplishments, and steps toward accomplishment—for every student.

The Need for Independence

Seventh-grader Mike announced, "Mr. Berckemeyer, all these writing topics are dumb. I can think of a hundred better topics. I want to come up with my own."

Ahhh . . . young adolescents! They crave freedom. They want to be independent from authority. They are capable of and eager for a good deal of independent learning. They've gained skills that help them tackle real-life, complex problems. And developmentally, they are ready for more autonomy in their own learning. When their learning activities include a good deal of independence, they will be much more engaged and invested in the learning.

Yet, independence means responsibility, and that can be downright daunting. Always maintain empathy for the scariness of independence, but nurture and consistently expect independence to help them move away from dependence on the teacher. Autonomy ignites passion and sparks creativity. Students are empowered when they know and appreciate their own strengths and when they have safe, guided chances to self-direct their behavior and follow their goals and interests independently. Here are some ideas to nurture students' independence:

- Start with an environment that breeds trusting relationships. Students who feel comfortable, have a sense of belonging, and trust the teacher and each other do best at taking responsibility for their own learning.

- Help students identify and appreciate their individual learning styles, strengths, and talents.

- Set up many opportunities where they can find information on their own; synthesize, analyze, and evaluate the information and the sources; use different media and approaches to share information and conclusions; and identify and solve real-life problems.

- Provide and practice tools and tips for organization and time management; these are foundational to independence. Cover this with daily planners, notices on websites or reminders on cell phones, calendars, organized binders, or assignment notebooks.

- Always set a purpose for their independent learning, or have them set the purpose. Make the assignment clear. Make sure they understand where they are going and have set their own learning goals.

- Give students checklists or other written reminders of the purpose, goals, resources available, and timelines. Keep these aids visible so they can proceed without asking, "What are we doing?" or "What is the assignment?" or "How much time do we have?"

- Whet their appetites to learn something new; then give them access to materials and the necessary time to explore and create and to share what they learned.

- Provide students with meaningful choices in classroom life. Offer frequent choices in problems, questions, learning tasks, classroom responsibilities, test questions, homework assignments, ways to learn, ways to show what they've learned, and ways to evaluate their learning.

- Offer plenty of opportunities for individuals to follow their own interests and passions in learning activities.

- Allow for mistakes, false starts, poor choices, and some wasted time. This is part of independent learning. Continue to have conversations about the skills for independent learning. Talk about mistakes and what they learned from them, why time was wasted, what choices would have been better, and what they'll do differently next time.

- Check in as they are working. Ask questions that keep them focused on their goals.

- Plan many opportunities for students to explain their own learning approaches and progress.

- Give them time and strategies for evaluating their own learning processes ("How did I go about solving this problem"? "What did I do to learn about this topic?") and their own achievement ("Did I meet my goals?" "What worked well?" "What did I do best?" "What confused me?" "What more do I need to learn?" "What would I do differently?")

- Find ways to enthusiastically celebrate what they've learned and how they've accomplished it independently!

- Avoid the temptation to control everything or to rush in to the rescue.

- Encourage and give reassurance with comments such as "You've got good ideas. Just follow one of them," "You know how to do this," or "I trust you to find the information you need," but then gently fade into the background. Of course, notice the student who really does need help and only give enough help to keep him or her moving forward independently.

The Need to be Heard

If you've been in a middle school or high school classroom for five minutes, you've heard some cryptic (or smart aleck), probably slightly (or grossly) inappropriate, adolescent comments.

Akin to the need for independence is the young adolescent's need to be heard. That need is deeper than just an attempt to grab attention with a wisecrack or shocking comment. Students need their most serious, important ideas to be heard. They also need their tentative or off-the-wall "wonderings" to be heard. When they feel that their ideas and opinions matter, they are empowered to take more control of their learning activities. This increases engagement in their learning, deepens their connection to other members of their learning community, and boosts their confidence as learners. And by the way, when students regularly experience a welcoming environment for their voices, the need to insult, shock, or wisecrack diminishes.

Take stock of your current classroom attitudes and practices to find ways to increase student opportunities for greater voice. Here are some signs that students' voices are valued in the classroom:

Students:
- Have chances to be heard without fear of being ignored, criticized, or ridiculed.

- Get frequent opportunities to express themselves with words, actions, art, media formats, and other creative means.

- Are actively involved in discussion and creation of classroom (or team) policies and procedures.

- Help to develop criteria and expectations for learning tasks.

- Take part in designing their own learning goals.

- Help to design strategies and instruments for evaluation of their work.

- Participate in evaluation of their own work and progress.

- Have many chances and choices for teaching, demonstrating, or otherwise showing what they have learned.

- Share and compare their thinking processes.

- When asked, will say their voices are heard and taken seriously.

Teachers:

- Regularly ask students for input into classroom events, projects, homework, curriculum, assignments, schedules, and management.

- Seriously listen to student input and use it.

- Include students in designing lessons and many kinds of learning activities.

- Arrange for student-led conferences where students describe their processes, progress, and needs.

- Give frequent opportunities for leadership development.

- Regularly use students as resources to help, teach, or advise others—including the teacher.

The Need for Feedback

We all need to know how we are doing as we learn or complete any task. Feedback helps brains learn. You see or hear what works, what doesn't work, and what you need to try again or change. Just watch a teenager play a video game. You'll see the barrage of instant feedback along with the player's quick adaptations to do a better job of meeting the game's goals. This increases engagement and motivation. Young adolescents are used to feedback. In their highly technological world, it's expected. Digital games and apps give instant feedback. Give students chances for that kind of regular feedback in the classroom. You can write it, say it, give it on a sticky note, or highlight something that meets a goal. Feedback can be in the form of words, symbols, or numbers on a scale. It can come from a teacher, peer, or computer program. In whatever form the feedback is given, make use of these bits of advice:

- The purposes of feedback are to learn something or strengthen skills. Feedback should be intended for positive results and always given in a positive spirit. The purpose is to uplift, never to tear down.

- Give feedback *soon* after the lesson, task, or event, while there is still time to act on it. Make sure the feedback suggests next steps for the student. And most important, give students time and ways to put the feedback to use right away

- Most of the time, feedback should be private so as to keep the anxiety, embarrassment, and threat levels low for students

- When students know criteria ahead of time, a good part of the feedback process is already underway. If they have a checklist or rubric or other example of what constitutes a successful performance, feedback will be quick to get or give to others.

- Give feedback to one skill or one part of the assignment. Too much feedback at once just dissipates into the universe.

- Avoid general feedback (and avoid repeating the same feedback). Such comments as "That's great!" "Good job!" "Nice work!" "Bravo!" don't teach the student anything. They sound hackneyed and students soon experience them as insincere.

- Give specific feedback. Use such targeted compliments, comments, questions, and suggestions as:
  —"I noticed that you used dialogue really well to show the personalities of your characters."
  —"That was a smart idea to check your problem solution using a different strategy."
  —"The alliteration really drew my attention to the opening line of your poem!"
  —"Were you as surprised as I am by the outcome of your experiment? Why?"
  —"Your side-by-side timelines show so many similarities in the history of these two events!"

- Teach students the art of feedback with the goal of them taking on more self-assessment and offering feedback to peers. Give students many chances and vehicles for reflecting on their progress. Provide ways for them to examine how they operate and how they think. Teach them ways to evaluate their work and to set goals for future work based on their self-evaluations.

- Teach students how to give and receive feedback constructively, positively, and kindly. Practice this.

The Need for Technology

The everyday lives of our young adolescent students are permeated with devices, games, and digital communication. Technology is not something that gets added to their lives by the use of a computer or laptop lesson in class—not anymore! It is part of the being of every young adolescent. Some schools don't have the technology they need.

Others overuse technology. Yes, I believe technology can be overused at school! Experts are recommending limits on screen time for children (Summers, 2014). So certainly students shouldn't be in front of screens for entire school days, right?

We must involve students with whatever technological tools are available. This does not mean, however, that everything students do in a classroom has to be technological. There are plenty of human and academic skills that do not use gadgets.

Balance—this word has to be part of the discussion about technology in classrooms. Students need learning experiences that keep them moving, manipulating and tinkering, discussing face-to-face, and creating with a multiplicity of materials—not all digital.

But, yes, to engage students in realistic, relevant learning experiences, and to manage students in twenty-first century classrooms, technology must be integrated. There are many good reasons for students to use the tools and skills that are parts of their present and future lives, learning, and jobs. And there are literally thousands of good resources (websites, apps, programs) available to help teachers design all kinds of educational activities using technology. These resources come and go daily. It is hard to imagine what will be out there even by the time you get this book! So:

- Don't hand a tablet to a student just so you can say you're using technology. Design tech-based activities purposefully. Be clear to yourself and students about the curriculum connection. As with any experiences you plan, identify the learning goals, the skills or processes to be used, and the means by which they will be accomplished, monitored, and assessed.

- Use smartphones, cameras, tablets, virtual reality gizmos, computers, projectors, smartwatches, digital music players, and any other devices available. Students need to practice the skills of operating the devices and applying what they know about one device to learn the technical aspects of new devices that come along rapidly.

- Provide and encourage activities for young adolescent students to communicate and work collaboratively with peers and with people in many parts of the world. Check out opportunities for virtual reality learning experiences (a growing curricular niche) to take students into other parts of the world and promote awareness of other cultures. Investigate the website of the *Global*

Nomads Curriculum (2017) and a 2017 article from *The Hechinger Report* about virtual reality in the classroom (Berdik).

- Create opportunities for students to build digital media literacy (also called multiple literacies) in using different formats and technologies. This means: give them chances to use technology to read, write, calculate, design, produce, devise, construct, communicate, research, and share. Digital literacy also includes the ability to manage, understand, integrate, interpret, analyze, synthesize, and critically evaluate content and sources.

- We must teach students to handle the information from media. Put students' cognitive skills to work as they deal with the overabundance of information and messages that come to them through the growing media sources. In addition to being able to take in information, they must have many guided experiences searching, finding, and critically evaluating sites, sources, and ideas. They must learn to make reasoned decisions and judgments about everything that is bombarding them. Give students lots of practice with these skills. They should be critically examining messages from movies, videos, song lyrics, website articles, digital and media advertisements, blogs, text messages, tweets, and many other media sources.

- Get familiar with the ISTE (International Society for Technology in Education) standards for students. Find the latest standards and many teaching resources at www.iste.org.

- Join with your staff to plan professional development sessions on the wise use of technology in the classroom. Two of my favorite tech consultants are Dedra Stafford and Chris Toy. I've watched them work many times and know that either one would be a great asset to your school. (See www.dedrastafford.com and www.christoy.net.)

- For yourself, make use of the many sites and apps that make classroom organization and activity management easier. Get to know the programs and sites that help you and students create flashcards, games, and quizzes; arrange and rearrange groups or seats; manage assessment; or communicate with students, parents, and colleagues.

- And, of course, follow all the policies and procedures of your school and your good sense as students are involved with technology-based sources. Teach, reteach, reinforce, and yes, even nag about, personal safety and privacy, respectful communication, protecting reputations, and appropriate Internet behavior. Engage students in continuous conversation about etiquette, ethics, and dangers of this media-technology world. Teach students to respect others' rights to privacy and to understand boundaries against stealing others' ideas, data, or music.

The Needs for Relevance and Authenticity

The classroom is enmeshed with a wider community that extends beyond the classroom doors and school corridors. Quite simply, the learning experiences—academic, personal, social, or emotional—must connect to your students' lives. This is what good teachers observe and what research confirms: engagement among students is increased when meaningful connections are made amongst schoolwork, the student's world outside of school, and the student's personal and academic goals (Assor, Kaplan, & Roth, 2002).

This is a no-brainer, right? We all know this. Without these two needs met, our young adolescent students won't be engaged in their learning. But with the thick curriculum guides, reams of standards, and tomes of content, we have to be on our toes and supremely savvy to actually make this happen regularly. To meet the needs for authenticity and relevance, we must:

- Motivate students with authentic events; real-world problems; things actually happening in their school, social groups, or community; actual questions they have; and real dilemmas they face. Pay attention to the news and current events. Help them see how what they are learning relates to developments around them. Use real events to help broaden their engagement with the wider world.

- Know and use students' interests as content for their learning. They love to talk about movies, videos, music, celebrities, scandals, and a host of real-world events. They know all the time what's in, what's out, what's new, what's old, what's trending, what's getting buzz, and what to watch online. They know what happened two seconds ago in some celebrity's life.

- Build lessons around their concerns, hopes, dreams, fads, and experiences. Find out what they are passionate about. Find out what motivates them. Then tap into their passions and intrinsic motivations. Always be aware of who the kids are and what they're thinking about. (Okay, so there are some things they are thinking about that you may not want to know.)

- Remember that young adolescents are egocentric. They evaluate concepts—and indeed everything—with themselves at the center of the world. Constantly ask them, "What difference does this idea make?" "How does it play out in the world?" "Where have you seen this idea or process at work in your life?" Always connect concepts, skills, processes, and content to their lives, to how what they've learned will affect them, or how they can use it.

- Transfer things they learn to other scenarios and experiences. Help them discover how a reading skill, math strategy, science discovery, art technique, or historical lesson is useful in something that happened outside their door, or in another culture, or in a completely different context.

- Learn their skills, strengths, and abilities. Design learning experiences where students can put their individual abilities to work—be it comedy, sculpture, coding, rapping, cooking, or fixing a broken air conditioner.

- Let your students teach you. You don't have to have all the information or know all the games, topics, and trends that interest them. Ask them. Let them be the experts on their subject matter. This gets them engaged. And just knowing that you want to learn from them is a huge boost to their trust in you.

The Need for Humor

Yes, I've mentioned humor before. But here I want to reinforce it again in the context of good teaching that engages students. I'd suggest that for every lesson, you have in your pocket (or drawer, or mind) a joke, a good anecdote, a costume, a gimmick, a prop, or other surprising, fun element. Take advantage of all the benefits of humor that help students relax, get hooked on the lesson, and retain information longer!

The Need for Your Presence

Part of engaging students in learning is engaging with them yourself. BE there. Move among them. Earlier in this chapter, I said teachers should roam while students are working in groups. That teachers should be on the move is a universal truth—for all activities. Your presence fosters their self-management and independence. To stay engaged in meaningful learning, students need you to be present. Not standing in one spot leaning against the wall, surveying the group. Not catching up on your email or texting the teacher down the hall while pretending to walk around. Not furtively working at your desk on a grad school paper or making lesson plans for the substitute.

This advice might seem simple and boringly obvious. But I'm in lots of classrooms, and I have to say that I still observe teachers looking down and never leaving one spot for much of a class period. You'd be surprised how many times teachers miss "interesting social behaviors" when they look down, even briefly.

I admit to starting my own teaching career head down and lost. It took weeks for me to learn that, to see everything, I had to ignore the ugly carpeting and look around the room. When I finally learned to stay on my feet, it got even worse, because I thought the whiteboard needed me and I rarely left its side.

When I finally began moving around the classroom, I became a better teacher. My presence among them helped calm insecure students, kept easily distracted students on task, alerted me about who was lost or confused, and let me catch students before they completely disengaged. I didn't miss a thing transpiring in the room. As you know, issues can crop up at the speed of light, and you need to witness every event and know the backstory. A favorite tactic of mine for staying engaged with students is to have them stand up when I stop by to chat. I don't like looking down on students and this approach puts the two of us on equal footing. It also gives the kid a chance to move and stretch.

So keep your head up! This will sharpen your visual and perceptual skills. Who knows? You might actually develop eyes in the back of your head. By the way, if you're addicted to sticking with your equipment, as I was, turn the projector, computer, or whiteboard responsibilities over to a student. This keeps that student focused! (I recommend choosing the student who is least likely to be paying attention when you're managing those tasks.)

The need for your presence extends beyond the classroom. You might think they're glad to get away from you. But as I pointed out in Chapter 2, young adolescents like the connection. Leaving school one day in a hurry to get to a doctor's appointment, I thought I heard my name as I raced across the parking lot. Sure enough, when I looked back, one of my students was hanging out of the school bus window wildly waving his hands. When he saw me look, he shouted, "Goodbye Mr. Berckemeyer . . . and you're a dork!"

I translated this to myself: "Mr. Berckemeyer, I care about you deeply. But I don't know how to articulate it."

The Boredom Factor

A typical dream for a teacher is to see every student in the class sitting on the edge of his or her seat anticipating knowledge on a daily basis. Not all students actually cooperate with the dream. No matter how hard you prepare for the lesson, no matter how many things you blow up or dissect, there will always be that one student (especially in a class of young adolescents) who says, "We did this last year, and this is boring. I hate this class."

Some students pretend they were born bored. Often it's not perceived as cool to love school or even to like a particular class or lesson. Yes, this means that your students will not get excited about the cool multicolored tiles (or even multicolored balloons) for math. But it does not mean that you should stick with fill-in-the-blank handouts or rows of written math problems. Just don't be surprised when your students fail to react the way you hoped.

This is critical to remember: the attitude of some of your students should not dictate your mood, the mood you allow to permeate the entire class, or the teaching strategies you choose. If a few students say they think the activity is stupid or boring, certainly don't let them change what you planned to do for a lesson. Tell them to sit out a while. Then keep everyone else busy doing a cool activity.

When young adolescents get bored, they look for ways to entertain themselves. Usually this involves someone nearby; they tend to poke, pull, or trip anyone who gets near them. A popular way to alleviate boredom is the my-pencil-is-not-sharpened-enough routine, which can be performed while you are teaching or working with a small group, during silent reading, or a quiz, or at any other time during the class period. The student gets up and walks toward the pencil sharpener, making a few stops along the way to disrupt others by knocking their papers on the floor, messing with their hair, or even giving them a slight shove. Having arrived at the pencil sharpener, the student makes as many attempts as needed to get the pencil sharp enough to use as a dart. Then the student begins the long journey back to his or her seat—this time using a different route and causing disruptions and distractions in a different part of the room.

Commit to a classroom where no student is bored and no one falls asleep or needs to wander around. Do this by keeping them hopping, moving, thinking, interacting, and doing. Give regular and appropriate brain breaks. Use a variety of strategies targeted to meet their needs and multiple learning styles. Be aware, however, that some students use the "I'm bored!" phrase as a habit to get attention, annoy you, or get a rise out of other students. Often they are not bored at all—just needing to be noticed. Still, keeping them engaged in fun, meaningful activities can erase even that habit.

> Adapting your teaching methods to match the range of young adolescents' characteristics and needs can, at times, be frustrating because their abilities and strengths are as varied as their shoe sizes and change just as fast.

Match Strategies to Development

A Teacher Activity

This chapter has focused on the idea that an engaging environment for young adolescents is grounded in the realities of their developmental needs and characteristics. The following activity gives you a way to envision specific experiences that connect to those. Using a form such as the one shown in Figure 4-1 ("Developmentally Responsive Teaching"), join with colleagues or teammates to create a list of ideas to match strategies to students' development. Include things you already do that you believe will work. But notice where there are gaps or weaknesses in your usual practices and challenge yourself to integrate new ideas and strategies. You might borrow ideas from some imaginative sources such as Jill Spencer's book *Everyone's Invited! Interactive Strategies that Engage Young Adolescents* (2008).

Select 15 or more of the items. Commit to implementing one powerful idea to embrace that characteristic or need. Set goals and timelines for the strategies. After trying each, make notes showing your experiences and evaluations of how it succeeded.

Figure 4-1 *Developmentally Responsive Teaching*

List strategies, lessons, or ideas that relate to the characteristics and needs of young adolescents.

Characteristic or Need	Example of Activity or Strategy
Rapid growth changes	
Struggle with self-esteem	
Intense curiosity	
Self-absorption	
Recognition seeking	
Developing new beliefs and attitudes	
Questions about moral and ethical issues	
Ability to see "shades of grey"	
Feel compassion for self and others	
Dealing with peer pressures	
Dealing with bullying and harassment issues	
Attraction to pop culture trends and fads	
Need for creative expression	
Need for self-definition	
Need for one-on-one time with teacher	
Need for time alone	
Need for positive peer relationships	
Need for structure and limits	
Need for time management and organization	

Figure 4-1 *Developmentally Responsive Teaching* *continued*

Characteristic or Need	Example of Activity or Strategy
Need to belong	
Need to feel normal	
Need for safety and security	
Need for social interaction in learning	
Need to move	
Need for concrete, active learning experiences	
Need for variety in learning experiences	
Need for familiarity in learning experiences	
Need for novelty in learning experiences	
Need for academic competence	
Need for independence	
Need for choice	
Need for own voice to be heard	
Need for feedback from self and others	
Need for technology	
Need for authenticity and relevance	

Source: *Managing the Madness: A Practical Guide to Understanding Young Adolescents and Classroom Management* © Association for Middle Level Education   www.amle.org

For Reflection and Action

1. After reading the section about the teacher being the main purveyor of the learning environment, list some of the behaviors, skills, or characteristics you model most consistently.

2. Is there anything that should be added to the paragraphs about the teacher's role in setting the tone for the learning environment (pp. 47–48)?

3. In what ways do you share your passion for teaching and for being with your students?

4. What ideas from the information about students working in groups did you find most helpful? What new ideas would you like to try?

5. For what characteristics or needs in the final activity (Figure 4.1) did you struggle the most to identify strategies?

6. Have a trusted colleague observe your body language while you teach. Do you tend to put your head down? Do you tend to stay in one place?

Source: *Managing the Madness: A Practical Guide to Understanding Young Adolescents and Classroom Management*
© Association for Middle Level Education   www.amle.org

CHAPTER 5

Of Manners and Other Social Skills

Mr. Berckemeyer, I can burp "The Star Spangled Banner."

In the last chapter I told you about a before-school experience in a coffee shop with a mob of young adolescents. What struck me in addition to the vast physical differences was their calm, respectful behavior. Honestly, there was no pushing and shoving, guffawing, posturing, or showing off. There were no subtle or blatant examples of rudeness. The kids spoke quietly, treated each other nicely, waited patiently for their turns, thanked the waitress, and cleaned up their messes. The boy who wanted to get a straw while I was taking up all the space at the little corner spot with the coffee accessories asked kindly, "Sir, is it okay if I reach around you to get a straw?" I couldn't imagine whom he was calling "Sir." Could I possibly look like a "Sir"?

However, last week at a mall food court, a horde of young adolescents rudely crowded out everyone else in line. They were loud and uncouth. They didn't acknowledge the presence of anyone over 16. They talked mean to each other. They left messes at their tables. And one day not long ago when a friend introduced me to her seventh-grade son, without looking at me (and with both hands in his pockets and wires from his ears mysteriously connected somewhere), he muttered, "Whassup?"

Just as young adolescents can be all over the map in development, so they can be in social skills. It does seem that manners have gotten lost these days. Perhaps it's because the bulk of teens' social interactions take place on devices and not face-to-face with live people. And those interactions are abbreviated, coded, full of slang, and have little room for common courtesies.

Plenty of adults have negative attitudes about teens. Some of this is a reaction to behavior that is boorish, dismissive, or appalling. How often have you been shocked by the language you hear on the school grounds? How often have you stood in the grocery store thinking, "I cannot believe parents allow their children to be this rude"? (By the way, did it ever occur to you to think, "I can't believe their teachers haven't taught them manners"?)

I don't want to jump on the "adolescents-are-awful" bandwagon, because I don't think they are. I see many examples of stellar and heartwarming social behavior. But there are also plenty of examples that point to apparent declines in decent social conduct. Whether your students are in need of crash interventions for their social skills or just could benefit from a bit more polishing of suitable behaviors, *know that the level of civility is a major factor in classroom management.* If social skills are downright rude or even somewhat crude, I can guarantee this: it will be nigh unto impossible to have the kinds of relationships and the great engaging academic experiences that lead to a productive learning environment.

> From what I see in the real world, most people that get fired don't lose their jobs for being too smart (our usual priority for education). They get fired for lying or for being rude, lazy, or just a jerk (things we often neglect to address).

Keep these three things in mind:

1. *Don't assume students come to you having the social skills they need.* They've probably heard plenty of messages about respect, kindness, and manners at home and at school. But a lot of factors keep students from acting in ways consistent with what they should have learned by this age. These are such factors as lack of practice in proper social behavior, inconsistency in the enforcement or reinforcement of it in many settings, the natural push-back against rules or norms that comes with adolescence, and the HUGE influence of peers and media messages in setting different norms for behavior.

2. *Social skills can be taught, and should be taught*, not just at the beginning of the year with a set of rules on the wall and in the student handbook, but constantly, persistently, and all year long. Create targeted lessons and activities to teach, discuss, and practice all kinds of social skills. There are unlimited opportunities to do this in classrooms and throughout schools. Watch for them! Use them!

3. *The "rules" for teaching social behavior seem to change when a teacher crosses the doorstep into middle school.* In the elementary grades, teachers have the attitude of being helpers or coaches on this life journey of learning and practicing decent social behavior. They make it fun. They remind gently. They know kids are learning, won't remember, have underdeveloped moral and behavioral sensibilities, and will mess up. The kindergarten, first-grade, or second-grade teacher sweetly sings, "Who's got a pencil?" and students sing back, "I've got a pencil!"

   By sixth grade, the teacher is barking, "Bernice! Where's your pencil?!" In middle school and high school, the "coach" seems to turn into the "uniformed enforcer of rules."

Respect

Social skills start with and revolve around this *r.e.s.p.e.c.t.* word in action. All students and adults deserve to spend their school days within a consistent culture of mutual respect. You can spot and feel mutual respect (or the lack of it) as soon as you walk into a classroom. You need only to watch and listen to the verbal and nonverbal interactions for a short while to sense the level of regard among the people in the room.

Just as the teacher is the number one model for what it looks like to be a serious and successful student, so the teacher is the main model for respectful relationships. Students must see, hear, and feel you respecting them and other students, their family members, and your colleagues. Kids can't hear you gossiping about or dissing someone on your phone and believe anything you then say about respect. You can't teach lessons about respect with much success if you make snide remarks about the principal or the teacher down the hall.

A strong message of Chapter 2 was the importance of teacher-student relationships. But it is not just the positive teacher-student relationships that are associated with greater student engagement, better attendance, higher achievement, and more desirable behavior. The hard work on relationships must extend to everyone in the classroom and the school. Students must perceive safety and support from each other—to have the greater sense of belonging, less loneliness, and the feeling of being valued that leads to motivation and comfortable participation.

So your job in respect to respect goes beyond modeling it. Make head-on engagement with respect as important as the subjects you teach:

- Ask students to define the word *respect*, give examples of it, and identify how they can tell when they see it (or don't see it). Continue to regularly define it, explain it, elaborate on it, discuss it, expect it, and respond to it with affirmation. Role-play situations to help students learn respectful behavior and communication.

- Clearly define *disrespect*. As you all live in a classroom together, plainly identify examples of disrespect. Continue to talk about attitudes, behaviors, words, gestures, body stances, facial expressions, and tones of voice that show respect or disrespect. With practice, students will become skilled at recognizing these.

- As early as the first day of school, emphasize that the school is focused on helping students learn and gain strength in positive, collaborative ways. Let them know that the intent is for the class to lift everyone up (as opposed to doing things that put people down). Do activities the first day that begin to build respect and togetherness.

- Commit to, talk about, encourage, and reinforce this message—a message that needs to come from students as well as you: "Everyone belongs in this classroom. Everyone is needed, important, included, and valued. We are ALL in this together. Everyone speaks about and relates to everyone else with regard. We all stick up for each other. This classroom is home to every student here and every student deserves to be secure in it."

- Together with your team members or other colleagues, voice and demonstrate this message constantly: "You are all OUR students!" No teacher should be heard using the labels "those kids" or "Mr. Berckmeyer's kids."

- Plan and continue multiple experiences for students to collaborate, help each other, learn about one another, compliment each other, and boost one another.

- Do not tolerate disrespect in any form: name-calling, labeling, belittling, stereotyping, sarcasm, teasing, shaming, or gossiping.

- Literally help students rephrase comments that border on disrespect (or cross the border), thus giving them alternatives to these comments. When you hear, "She is a XXXXX," translate it into "She is having a difficult day." Even better, teach students to ask themselves, "How can I respond in ways that respect or help?"

- Actively honor everyone's privacy, feelings, opinions, interests, accomplishments, learning styles, and differences.

Manners (aka Social Graces)

Okay, I know. You're not teaching at a charm school. And you're not Ms. (or Mr.) Manners or Emily Post. And you have lots of complicated content to teach. But think about this: you can't survive in a classroom (not with a modicum of sanity, that is), nor can your students, without some practice of civility.

If you ask a group of adolescents, "What are the benefits of using good manners?" the most frequent answer might be, "So we don't get into trouble."

Pier Forni, a professor at Johns Hopkins University and author of bestsellers *The Civility Solution: What to Do When People Are Rude* (2009) and *Choosing Civility: The Twenty-five Rules of Considerate Conduct* (2003), has studied the significance of civility, manners, and politeness in contemporary society. He says, "The rules of good manners are the traffic lights of human interaction. They make it so that we don't crash into one another in everyday behavior" (2003, p. 7).

I like to tell students, "Manners allow people to live together without embarrassing themselves and each other."

Most of your lessons on manners will emerge naturally from the ordinary behaviors and interactions that go on when a group of people lives together. You teach these by what you say, how you act, how you respond, what you expect, and what you allow. You grab teachable moments and throw in good advice throughout the class. So this section of the chapter does not ask you to add a whole new topic to your curriculum. However, given the benefits of civility, it's worth taking some time for specific, planned situations to practice things like kindness, etiquette, compassion, fairness, patience, and honesty. Here are some ideas for dealing with the topic of manners:

- Ask students to think about the reason for manners or the benefits of manners. You'll get some quirky, slapstick ideas. But you'll probably be surprised at students' insights. You might give them the above three quotes about reasons for manners and ask them to compare and discuss them.

- Teach them the word *civility*. You can even build a writing, speaking, discussion, reading, or social studies lesson around this topic. Students can find examples of civility (or lack thereof) in historical or current events.

- Never underestimate the power of your example. Place high regard on politeness. Model the following practices with committed regularity: Say "hello" brightly and kindly to everybody. Say "please" and "thank you" to students. And greet every student who enters your room—every day!

- Students may resist any talk of manners. Nevertheless, they are taking in what you say, teach, and do. Find opportunities to model, discuss, role-play, or weave into lessons examples and situations related to:
  — Saying "please," "thank you," and "you're welcome"
  — Not interrupting
  — Saying "excuse me" when you need attention
  — Saying "excuse me" when you bump into someone
  — Diminishing the spread of your germs
  — Using courteous ways to get attention
  — Asking permission
  — Not whining or complaining
  — Not acting bored (even if you are)
  — Not eating in sloppy, gross, or offensive ways
  — Not contributing gross sounds or smells to the classroom
  — Not using appropriate language (no cursing)
  — Stifling insults, negative opinions, put-downs
  — Keeping your hands to yourself
  — Looking people in the eye when conversing
  — Respecting people's personal space
  — Respecting the privacy of others' belongings
  — Apologizing when you are wrong

- Be honest with students about inappropriate social behaviors. You might have to talk about some "weird" stuff or mention behaviors you'd like to avoid mentioning. Young adolescents need straight talk from adults who don't shy away from realities of uncouth behaviors. Discuss and practice appropriate alternatives.

- Ask them to use your full last name. Don't let them start the practice of calling you just by your title ("Hey teacher," "Hey, Ms.," or "Hey, Mr.") or by any nicknames.

- Young adolescents seem to run into each other a lot. Some of this is about their rapidly growing, unfamiliar, awkward bodies. But it's not polite. Often it is intentional and downright rude or mean. Notice when this happens. Stop the pushing or bumping right there and then, and use it as an occasion for them to practice appropriate apologies.

- Teach students about other occasions for apologies. When a conflict has been settled, handshaking and some sort of apologetic or reconciling words give closure to the situation. Teach them how to shake hands and make eye contact when apologizing (unless handshaking or eye contact is a cultural issue).

- Acknowledge students who do charity work and helpful deeds inside and outside school.

- If you have a recognition program (such as Student of the Month) that is based on special actions of care, courtesy, or other positive social skills, be sure to publicize and celebrate the honor. You can use such rewards and recognitions as giving coupons for a favorite fast-food restaurant; announcing names on the PA system; posting pictures on the hall bulletin board, in the school newspaper, or on the school website; or awarding special plaques. However, emphasize the meaning and competence that the student gains from the actions. These intrinsic rewards last longer than the snacks and badges.

- Discuss the topic of manners at a faculty meeting. Generate ideas for encouraging basic manners for all people in the school, including the adults.

- Initiate the development of a school-wide, classroom, or team policy on courtesy. Include students in this. Post the understandings in hallways and rooms.

Bullying

According to the U. S. Department of Education (2016), 20.8% of students ages 12 through 18 are regularly bullied at school—amounting to well over three million students a year. And 160,000 students stay home from school each day to avoid bullying (pp. T-1, T-21-26). Do the math: If almost 21% are regularly bullied, this means that at least that many are doing the bullying—making half of our students involved as bullies or targets. And the 20.8% is only what is reported!

Other surveys find such factors and statistics as:

- The majority of bullying incidents are not reported. (This makes so much sense to me. I'd wager that just about every middle school student has an experience with bullying.)

- Many teachers see little wrong with much of the bullying and only one in four regularly intervene.

- Over half of teens say they've been bullied online or on their cell phones.

- One in three teens report being threatened online.

- Peers intervene in bullying only about 10% of the time.

- After about age 10, kids don't regularly discuss bullying with their friends.

Bullying takes a huge emotional toll on victims, leaving deep and often lifelong scars. It leaves victims feeling vulnerable, powerless, terrified, and even depressed or suicidal. It's difficult to defend against being bullied or to repair the damage. Bullying is highly detrimental to the bullies as well. It generally comes out of needs and feelings that go unaddressed, and it often extends into long patterns of aggression, moral disengagement, troubled relationships, and even future "encounters" with the law.

School should be a safe place for all students. It is highly likely that your school has given serious attention to the problem of bullying and has clear policies regarding the matter. Most schools have a zero-tolerance policy toward bullying. Your primary approach with your students on the topic of bullying must be in line with and support of your school's policies.

You are smack in the middle of the bullying crises—right along with your students. As a teacher, you are the front line in courageously confronting bullying behavior. Make sure you:

- Know and consistently follow your school's anti-bullying policies.

- Regularly review and discuss these policies with students and hold students to them.

- Are clear with students about what bullying is. Too often they minimize or normalize bullying behavior. With all bullying, the intention is to hurt someone and usually the bullying is repetitive. Generally a bully selects someone perceived as weak or vulnerable to bully. Discuss all the forms bullying can take (below) but emphasize that bullying is any aggressive behavior that causes discomfort to someone else.

Physical bullying—This can include everything from pushing, shoving, and tripping to outright assault. It also includes damaging of property. This gets the most attention in schools because it is most visible.

Verbal bullying—This often happens when adults are not around and includes such things as name-calling, intimidating, teasing, threatening harm, and insulting.

Social-emotional bullying—This is social-relational manipulation or action to hurt, threaten, embarrass, belittle, insult, or humiliate someone, or to sabotage someone's social status. It includes lying; spreading rumors; use of nonverbal signals, facial expressions, physical gestures, or nasty looks; playing mean jokes; mimicking; breaking confidences; gossiping; ostracizing; and actively damaging reputations. Girls use this type of bullying more than boys.

Sexual bullying—This ranges from crude comments or vulgar gestures to unwelcome touching to sharing porn materials or "private" images and texts to propositioning to outright sexual assault. Girls participate in this by calling each other sex-related names such as "slut." The practice of sexting often leads to sexual bullying.

Prejudicial bullying—This bullying can take any of the forms above as bullies insult, threaten, or harm based on race, religion, sexual orientation, disabilities, or specific group attachments or physical attributes.

Cyberbullying—This is a monumental and growing issue. Like prejudicial bullying, it can take many of the above forms. It is the use of technology to transmit hurtful texts, posts, images, emails, and responses. It includes the spreading of rumors, gossip, lies, and intimidation. It can include online exclusion. It's hard to combat because cyberbullies are generally anonymous. The anonymity lowers the risk of being caught and provides bullies a detachment that allows for great cruelty. They can pretend to be someone they are not. The bullying can happen around the clock. Some of the bullies harass and stalk; these can include strangers to the student (even adults pretending to be teens).

- Have lots of conversations about bullying. Have these when incidents related to bullying arise. Beyond that, plan specific ways to engage students on the topic. Talk about how subtle bullying can be. Ask students to describe bullying situations they have seen (with no names named) and times they have participated in bullying or stood by. Before incidents begin, discuss and practice bullying prevention and options for responding to bullying.

- Dive head-on into the very real problem of bystanders to bullying. Talk about why this happens and what the outcomes are. Make it clear that standing by encourages bullying. The person who forwards offensive messages or photos becomes a bully. The person who encourages the bullying by cheering, laughing, or otherwise accepting it also becomes a bully. More than 85% of bullying incidents on playgrounds and in classrooms are witnessed by bystanders (Storey, Slaby, Adler, Minotti, & Katz, 2013, p. 24).

- Promote the power of students standing up to bullying as a group. Talk about how standing alone against a bully is risky but when a group of students shows disapproval, bullies often back down. Get students to plan ahead for what ways they can respond when they see someone getting bullied. Wendy M. Craig and Debra J. Pepler (2000), who research the bullying topic, found that more than half the time, bullying stops within 10 seconds of a bystander stepping in to help. This includes peer bystanders (pp. 22-36). Wow! Talk about power! The *Eyes on Bullying* project of the Education Development Center encourages bystanders to stand up for the victim by saying something simple such as "Leave him alone" or "Stop" or "It's not funny" in a nonaggressive manner (Storey et al., 2013, p. 29).

- Don't ignore bullying. Intervene immediately and report it according to school-approved processes. Don't delay. It is not helpful to the bully to let incidents slide. And it's devastating to the victim. Don't leave the kids to "work it out" on their own. The *Eyes on Bullying* project reports that "adults intervened in only 4% of the bullying incidents they witnessed" on the playground (Storey et al., 2013), p. 29). Again, wow! This shakes me!

- In your responses, address bullies' needs and actions in addition to taking steps to protect the bullied. Help kids find reasons not to bully and to see rewards in kinder relationships. Help bullies learn and practice alternative behaviors.

- Talk about why people bully. Ask students for suggestions about this. Talk about the need to feel powerful and controlling, feel better about themselves, respond to their own experiences of social rejection or academic failure, increase their own social standing, and get attention or popularity.

- Repeatedly encourage students to report bullying. Review ways to do this, including options for confidential reporting.

- Stay informed. Share the information with other parents, colleagues, and students. There are hundreds of good resources for teachers, students, and parents that can help define, identify, understand, avoid, respond to, heal from, and combat bullying. I strongly recommend that you read and use the free *Eyes on Bullying Toolkit* from http://www.eyesonbullying.org/pdfs/toolkit.pdf.

Technology and Social Skills

Perhaps nothing has had as dramatic an effect on young adolescents' social skills as the explosion in the use of digital communication. To say they are ardent consumers of this technology is an understatement. They're voracious. Due to their portable mobile devices, they can be connected to friends, social networks, and a multitude of media information sources almost constantly. They have never known a world without Internet; they are at the most developmentally vulnerable age for its influence and dangers; and they are the heaviest users of social networking.

Parents and teachers can make long lists of risks and cautions related to technology use by young adolescents. A swelling body of research examines and publicizes risks, dangers, and areas of concern. With all the hours kids spend on screens, we worry about and SHOULD worry about:

- Their abilities to form and continue real relationships that actually involve the complexities and rewards of face-to-face interaction.

- The social misunderstandings that arise from communicating in a minimal number of characters and pictures. We know kids are stripped of the nuances and personal aspects of communication.

- What this is doing to their brain development, their inactive bodies, and their sleep patterns.

- Their possible disconnection from reality and from each other.

- The signs of digital addiction we see in our students and our own children.

- Perhaps most terrifying of all, the real dangers that lurk on social sites: cyberbullying, sexting, predatory behavior, trolling, catfishing, pornography, and the terrible emotional and physical ramifications of these.

If you research the effects of Internet or social media on teens and pre-teens, you'll also find long lists of benefits (intellectual, educational, social, emotional, and creative benefits). Digital connection gives them powerful ways to pursue interests, to give voice to their ideas, to organize activities, and to discuss and debate ideas far beyond their own communities and countries. They get opportunities to create, share content, get and give feedback, explore, collaborate, and meet others with similar interests. Kids can keep contact with parents and with friends near and far. They can search for help and information on sensitive topics (that are uncomfortable to discuss in person) and maintain support systems that would not be possible otherwise.

In a 2012 Common Sense Media research study of more than 1000 teens reporting on how they view their digital lives, researchers found that "teens are much more likely to report that using social media has a positive impact on their social and emotional lives than a negative one" (p. 10). Many teens reported feeling less shy, more outgoing, more confident, more popular, more sympathetic to others, better about themselves, and less depressed. More than half of teens surveyed said social media makes their relationships with friends better. Over a third believed that social media helps their relationships with family members, helps them get to know fellow students better, and increases their connections with new people who share common interests (p. 10).

It's perhaps easiest to start tallying up all the ill effects of technology. So I wanted to make three of my understandings about young adolescents and technology use clear:

It's in the fiber of our students (no escaping it); there are indeed recognized benefits; and we're nuts not to pay close attention to the real dangers.

Digital communication and consumption are deeply entangled with social skills and thus with classroom life. I'll summarize some factors that I see. Then I'll give a few (hopefully wise and helpful) ideas for responding to the factors.

I see that students' social skills are learned, used, refined, altered, or influenced:

1. By the sheer fact of the time they spend with devices.

2. By what they see and hear from technological sources (by the information and messages coming at them).

3. By what they do, say, and share digitally.

1. The Time They Spend

According to research from the Pew Research Center, 92% of American teens go online daily (many of them several times a day); 24% say they go online almost constantly; 75% have or have access to a smartphone; and only 12% report having no cell phone of any type. They exchange (on average) 70 texts a day—and most report that they text every day. They are heavy users of social network sites, generally using multiple sites, with the most popular currently being Instagram, Snapchat, Facebook, Twitter, and Google+ (Lenhart, Purcell, Smith, & Zickuhr, 2010; Lenhart, 2012).

A 2015 landmark study by Common Sense Media reported that 75% of American teenagers are registered on social networking sites and 13- to 17-year-olds spend an average of nine hours a day using media for entertainment (TV, online videos, gaming, Internet use, music, and social media—with 6.8 hours of that looking at screens). This does not include use for school or homework (pp. 9-10). According to this same study, "half of all teenagers say they are addicted to their digital devices" (pp. 9-10).

Yes, adolescents can watch TV, use social media, text, talk, and listen to music while doing their homework (and most think it has no effect on their work). They can carry on three different conversations without saying a single word out loud—and do this while you're teaching a lesson (unless you have strong controls over device use at school and perhaps even if you do)! Some of us struggle to remember the face-to-face conversation we had just 10 minutes ago or whether we sent the text message we pecked out on our phones. These multi-tasking kids can listen to the news reporter, attend to the updates scrolling across the bottom of the screen, notice the weather report on the side of the screen, and register the stock market highlights flashing elsewhere on the screen—and remember it all. Meanwhile, we have to hop up and get close to the screen to even see the scrolling updates!

Recently at an airport, I watched a young teenager playing a game on his smartphone while his parents were chatting with some other travelers about lost luggage and flight delays. What did he care about luggage or his parents' conversations? He didn't even seem to notice that the other family had a teenage boy of a similar age (also engrossed in some virtual firefight, pillaging of ships in pirate mode, stealing of cars in a fictional metropolis, or spawning of a hostile mob).

I'm sure you've watched a family at a restaurant "together" with kids on smartphones or tablets (and maybe parents, too) oblivious to the presence of the others. I'm sure you've wondered if there are any dinner conversations anymore that do not involve tweets. Okay, so it's one thing to ignore your parents. But I'm sure you've also watched a group of adolescents walking together—all glued to their devices. Are they texting each other? Do you know that many schools have stopped assigning homework so that families can actually have time together? And don't you know for sure that if there weren't strict rules in schools for cell phone use, you, the teacher, would be completely ignored in your classroom?

What IS the teacher to do?
Most of your students' "plugged-in" time is likely outside of school and out of your control. However, don't underestimate the ramifications of their digital activity on classroom relationships and management. There is plenty you can do to address this factor of the colossal amount of time they are connected and the ways it spills over into the classroom.

- Share with students some research (articles, videos, etc.) about the benefits and ill consequences of tech time. Use these texts for discussions and critical reading or thinking experiences related to your subject area.

- The 2012 Pew Research Center study mentioned earlier found that teens prefer face-to-face communication and know full well that social media can interfere. Some really wish they could be less addicted and would like help unplugging (Lenhart, pp. 11-12). Discuss with students the benefits and downsides of hyper connection. Let them brainstorm reasons for taking breaks from their phones and from media. Use class-related experiences to help them set goals for scaling back, for unplugging, and for increasing face-to-face communication. Help them appreciate the time in school that they are unplugged.

- Teach students to take good care of their own brains and development by practicing balance between various ways of learning and connecting. Help them see the positive aspects of life offline.

- Plan situations where students can discuss ways their social media use and constant connection affect classroom life. Encourage them to brainstorm solutions for issues this creates.

- Watch your own tech-connected behavior in the classroom and around the school. Follow the same rules that students have to follow. Remember how important your example is. Are you addicted to your smartphone?

2. What They See and Hear Technologically

Every time our students are online or are using an app, they are bombarded with dozens of examples of social skills—good, bad, and ugly; appropriate and inappropriate; desirable and undesirable. Movies, TV, videos they watch on YouTube and other sites, images on sharing sites, messages on any social site—all these are full of attitudes, language, behaviors, manners, responses, and choices that give lessons about how to act, think, and behave. *Never underestimate how much the social behaviors they absorb digitally outside the classroom help to shape their social skills that show up in the classroom.*

Keep in mind what you know about the development of these young adolescents: They are highly impressionable. They are highly susceptible to examples set by celebrities and other role models. They have an insatiable need to know the latest trends, fads, gossip, and scandals. They want to know what's going on with all their peers. They think they're wise and invulnerable; so often they have no awareness that something going into their eyes, ears, and brains is inappropriate (or worse, harmful). They will even watch and read things that *they know* are inappropriate. They want to laugh at, retweet, and repeat stuff they see that is liked by peers (even if it is really dumb stuff)!

What IS the teacher to do?

I'll say again what I advised in Chapter 2: You have to *know* about these messages. As much as it might alarm or nauseate you, you must be aware of the kinds of messages your young adolescent students are consuming. Otherwise, you're disconnected from them. You're an object in the classroom like the pencil sharpener—maybe slightly useful, but mostly irrelevant to their lives.

All the adults in the lives of our students must do everything we can to help them develop skills, morals, and maturity to handle what they are consuming technologically. This means teaching and practicing critical awareness, analysis, and evaluation of it all.

- Don't shy away from the content of the music, video games, Internet, and all other popular media. *Use* what they are taking in as parts of your lessons. (Of course, you have to screen the language and images!) Start with a TV show, video, (cleaned up) concept or message from song lyrics, current hot news story, catchy advertisement, celebrity scandal, tweet, social media transmission or image, or video game. Ask students to identify:

  — What message is being communicated.
  — What social skills are shown.
  — What it says, shows, and implies about behavior.
  — What values are represented.
  — What is respectful or disrespectful and to whom.
  — Examples of fakery, discrimination, and insults.
  — Examples of honesty, care, inclusion, and tolerance.
  — How they would feel if the message were about them.
  — How the idea or message harms or helps them.

- Get students used to examining digital content constantly and with sharp brains and critical eyes. Make this fun. They'll be proud of how quickly they learn to do this. It will make them feel mature, smart, and independent.

- Create opportunities for students to discriminate between positive and negative or time-wasting uses of the Internet. Turn them on to research about the positive and negative outcomes from teens' Internet use, including video games and social media.

- Create opportunities for students to discern unreliable sites and fake information.

- Many young adolescents (particularly girls) check social media constantly to see what others are saying about them, to make sure they are not missing out on anything, or to compare themselves to others. Hold discussions about the anxiety this habit breeds. Get them talking about how they feel when they get no responses. Discuss ways to build independence from and resilience to the constant pressures of sending and getting messages and "likes".

- Students receive endless media and personal messages that show disrespect. Point this out. Help them to become automatic at noticing these. Help them understand that the more disrespect they see and hear—particularly from role models they admire or in forms that are entertaining and flashy—the more they become desensitized to disrespect. Your students are smart enough and old enough to see this and to work at keeping from being sucked into believing it is okay.

- Beyond watching out for disrespect, young adolescents need to be trained to be constantly alert for messages that are bullying, pornographic or otherwise inappropriate, mean-spirited, or dangerous. Help them learn how to spot and what to do about cyberbullies, trolls, and other online fakes and dangers.

- Encourage students to have the good sense and courage to log off when anything is uncomfortable, vulgar, inappropriate, personal, or threatening. Help them learn the kinds of messages that they should report to an adult.

- Find multiple and regular opportunities for students to reflect on the cumulative effects of always being digitally connected. Get them talking about what they miss that could be rewarding or instructive for them personally. Learning to make choices about how, when, when not, why, and why not to use technology is a critical skill for young adolescents.

3. What They Do, Say, and Share Digitally

Young adolescents fervently want to belong. They want to be like their peers. They want to feel popular. They want to know what their peers are saying and doing online. They want to make and keep friends. They want to be seen as attractive, clever, fun, and "in the know." They want to feel important and included. They want validation and connection. They want to get attention and approval. They want to gain status. They want to compare themselves to others. They want to share themselves, their pictures, their activities, their ideas, and their opinions. They like instant sharing and instant feedback. The "likes" they get on social media are intoxicating. Positive responses to their posts boost their self-esteem. Participation in social media, games, and other online activities makes all this possible.

Our adolescent students are putting themselves out there—way out there—all the time. They are posting, commenting, sending image after image, sharing, and over sharing. It's no secret, even to them, that they divulge far more digitally than they would face-to-face. Because of all this sharing, there is a serious amount of information that our students need to know and behaviors they should practice to be safe, courteous, ethical, and legal in digital activities.

What IS the teacher to do?

As I mentioned above, most of the personal tech communication is done outside your classroom. But students need to understand that the social skills learned in the classroom must extend to all parts of their lives.

- Many of the reasons technology use is so pervasive for our students flow directly from their normal adolescent needs. One obvious way for us as teachers to relate to this is to address these same needs in the classroom. This means giving students plenty of ways offline (face to face) to develop relationships, polish social skills, receive validation, get feedback, satisfy their needs to belong, and share their creations, ideas, and opinions.

Now I'm not dense enough to think offline activities will diminish their digital output. But it just could help to balance the ways their needs get met.

- Reinforce the following message to students as often as possible: "What you say, do, and share online makes a difference. It affects your lives. If affects the lives of others."

- Students have heard this and think they know this—but repeat this anyway: "If it's online, it's public. If it's online, it's forever." This pertains to Internet use in school and out of school.

- Repeat and reinforce the following non-negotiable safety rules. This pertains to Internet use in school and out of school:

- Give no personal information online.
- Post no personal images online without parental permission.
- Post no images of anyone else online without their permission.
- Give no information about your parents online.
- Give no personal information about anyone else online.
- Fiercely guard your privacy and the privacy of others.
- Never meet anyone in person that you meet online.
- Never give your password to anyone.
- Never open links from people or sources you don't know.
- Never comment to or interact with bullies or trolls. LOG OFF IMMEDIATELY.
- Talk to an adult about anything that happens online that makes you feel uncomfortable.

- Information about students' tech communications must be taught or reinforced in the classroom. Plan direct, explicit instruction and lots of discussion on topics related to the real consequences (positive and negative) of what and how they share or respond. Include such topics as:
  - Dangers of posting photos
  - Moral, personal, and legal consequences of posts
  - Pretending to be someone you are not
  - Dangers of making comments on "public" sites

- Have students investigate and discuss various definitions of "digital citizenship." They can go on to evaluate the quality of their patterns and actions related to digital communities and digital content.

- Discuss and practice online manners. These manners should hold for all online use, including for school activities.
  - Be polite at all times.
  - Voice your opinion respectfully.
  - Respect others' points of view.
  - Respect the privacy of other's devices.
  - Stay off your devices while talking to someone in person.
  - Put your devices away during meals and performances.

— Friend and unfriend people kindly on social media sites.

— Don't add your comments to online arguments.

— Use emogis courteously.

— Wait and re-read any message before hitting "send."

— Don't tag pictures with friends' names without permission.

— DON'T be a cyber bully. Before you send or forward a message or comment, ask yourself: "Is this going to hurt anyone?" "Is there anything threatening, gossiping, teasing, excluding, or insulting about this?" and "How would I feel if I got this message?"

— Don't forward any messages of the kind mentioned above.

— Use your digital time and skills to promote positive relationships and connections. Speak up for kindness, challenge stereotypes, and embrace diversity.

Some Other Social Skills

Other skills that have to do with life inside and outside of school are appropriate to address and practice in school. These are such skills as how to:

- Talk to each other
- Talk to adults
- Meet and greet people
- Advocate for yourself and others
- Ask for help
- Behave in public places
- Be ready to learn in this and other classrooms
- Show compassion, caring, and empathy
- Give and receive compliments
- Listen well
- Behave and work in groups
- Trust and be trustworthy
- Cooperate
- Be fair

- Be humble
- Help others
- Develop and handle relationships
- Be a friend
- Make decisions
- Participate in thoughtful discussion and debate

Other social skills that fall into the category of self-regulation or self-management also merit classroom time and attention. Plan explicit instruction, experiences, and time to practice:

- Handling anger
- Dealing with anxiety or fear
- Responding to peer pressure
- Improving attitudes
- Being resilient
- Overcoming obstacles
- Being persistent
- Identifying and accepting strengths and weaknesses
- Controlling behavior
- Developing self-awareness and self-worth

Every educator wants students to be kind, caring, and respectful. But that may not always be possible with young adolescents. Part of growing up is to break some of the traditions and expectations handed down by adults. Young adolescents naturally push buttons and experiment with rude behaviors. However, with some monitoring, reminding, gentle correcting, and a lot of role modeling they will figure out proper ways to act. Celebrate incidences of good respect, good manners, and helpful deeds. Celebrate situations where the group does a good job together of inclusion, equity, listening to each other, respecting different viewpoints, honoring privacy, or combatting bullying. Be hopeful about your students improving and even polishing social skills. It just takes practice, time, and consistency.

For Reflection and Action

1. How would you rate your school's climate of civility? What issues do the faculty and administration need to address?

2. Set at least three goals for ways you can personally become a more effective model of social skills.

3. Keep a record of how many times you ignore or are tempted to ignore absolute no-no behaviors in your class or in the hallways.

4. What's the most successful strategy you've tried for promoting respect in your classroom? What's the best strategy you've witnessed from a colleague or other source? Make it a point to share best strategies with at least two other colleagues.

5. Step up your efforts to address the bullying topics and try bullying-related strategies from this chapter. Write a reflection about the results.

6. Describe the most striking student responses after you've had some of the discussions about technology-related social skills as recommended in this chapter.

Source: *Managing the Madness: A Practical Guide to Understanding Young Adolescents and Classroom Management*
© Association for Middle Level Education   www.amle.org

CHAPTER 6

Getting Ahead of the Madness

Mr. Berckemeyer, why are you looking at me like I'm about to do something wrong?

Scenario #1: Your day has been long. Your week has been longer with no outdoor breaks for students due to wet, miserable weather and multiple interruptions to the smooth plan you so thoughtfully crafted. With spring break just around the corner, students are particularly squirrely. And then Jacob shows up to last period class without the necessary book, notebook, or pencil—for the hundredth time. When you mention it, he's unusually mouthy and resistant. You've had enough. While seething aloud, "You're headed to the office!" you grab the paper to write the discipline referral. Your blood pressure is off the scale. Your left eye is twitching. Your right hand is shaking. You might even be considered irrational at this point. So you react to the problem.

Scenario #2: Just when you thought things were going well, something happened so quickly that you stood in a corner of your room muttering to yourself in awe, "All I did was say, 'Please move to a quiet place in the room for this next activity.' It seemed simple enough." And yet, the next thing you knew, three kids were pushing each other, two were crying, a fire had started, the lights were out, and a pyramid of chairs had appeared in the center of the room. How could this happen in only two minutes?" A straightforward transition turned into an impossible undertaking of trying to herd three dozen cats in the same direction. The cats were everywhere, shrieking, with claws out. You had no option here except to react.

We all get to this point once in a while. Unfortunately, too many teachers reach this point more than once in a while. Their management styles are heavily based on the practice of reacting to each problem as it comes up.

Reactive Management

The outstanding marks of reactive management are not anticipating what kinds of situations and behaviors might occur and not being ready for them. Because of this, many management issues in classrooms are actually caused by the teacher. Here are some ways teachers guarantee management problems:

- Let classroom arrangements contribute to disruptions and confusion.

- Get too busy teaching content to take time to reinforce respectful, trusting classroom relationships.

- Leave students with an incomplete or murky understanding of expectations.

- Make up consequences on the fly, i.e., give out consequences that students have not been told about beforehand.

- Get to class unprepared or only partially prepared.

- Address problems long after they occur (or not at all).

- Forget to use your knowledge of young adolescent development to inform your actions and decisions.

- Leave your passion back at your apartment and teach with little enthusiasm.

- Let learning activities become rote, repetitive, and less than engaging.

- Get around to grading assignments whenever you get around to them.

- Put up with unplanned, chaotic transitions from one activity to the next.

- Expect misbehavior from certain kids and give subtle or overt signs that show you expect it.

- Reprimand students in front of their peers.

- Punish the whole class for something one or a few students did.

- Let your consistent enforcement of policies slide.

A major component of reactive management is giving attention to students only when wrong choices are made. The teacher spends a lot of time handing out (or threatening to hand out) negative consequences. At best, the result is a hit-or-miss approach with occasional wise responses to a problem but with more responses that don't fix anything (or make things worse). This leads to insecurities and confusion for students. They can't count on the teacher to follow through on rules. They can't trust the teacher to handle problems consistently.

Reactive management is detrimental for students and their teachers. Researchers Penny Clunies-Ross, Emma Little, and Mandy Kienhuis (2008) studied the relationships among classroom management strategies, teacher stress, and student behavior. They found that in classrooms with predominantly reactive (as opposed to proactive) management styles, teachers were more stressed and students had less on-task behavior (pp. 693-710).

Proactive Management

Proactive management is the combination of intentional processes and strategies a teacher uses to

1. Prevent incidents and issues.
2. Lessen problem behavior that does occur.

Too often teachers think of classroom management only as discipline—as ways to handle misbehavior. Proactive management approaches the life of the classroom from a positive perspective. Teacher and students work together as a team to make the classroom a place where everyone is comfortable and safe, gets along, and is able to learn. The teacher predicts what problems are likely to arise and has appropriate responses planned.

If you're following practices such as those recommended in Chapters 1-5 of this book, you're already removing many causes of student misbehavior and are well on your way to a proactive management style. This chapter and the remaining chapters will add more strategies for proactive management.

When students are launching water-bottle rockets to learn about energy, force, and aerodynamics don't expect to have quiet and control.

Elements of Proactive Management

Here are some key components of proactive management:

Understanding the development and lives of young adolescents—The teacher has a firm grasp on the needs and characteristics of young adolescents, on their interests and passions, on the details of their youth culture, and on the stresses and pressures that they carry with them daily into the classroom. The teacher's plans for learning and living together in the classroom grow from this knowledge.

Knowing individual students well—The teacher understands the unique backgrounds and experiences of the students. He knows and accepts the diversity of backgrounds, home lives, and parent involvement that students bring with them to school. She knows that students deal with all kinds of complex situations at home and at school and that these can explain why a student disengages, doesn't bring materials to class, is crabby, or never finishes homework. The teacher is able to show empathy in ways that help the student feel understood.

Relationship building—Serious attention, discussions, teaching, and activities are dedicated to building appropriate, trusting teacher-student and student-student relationships. Teachers and students are in the habit of contributing to positive interactions every day.

Physical classroom environment geared for learning—The classroom is not cluttered or confusing. The arrangement and décor of the classroom are well planned to promote harmony, decrease problems, and spark learning

Humor—Humor is an intentional and present factor in classroom life. It's evident to students or visitors that the teacher has a sense of humor. The teacher integrates humor into learning activities, appreciates young adolescent humor, and helps students adjust their own humor appropriately to the classroom.

Structure—The teacher understands that even adolescent students need the structure that school offers and need to know that predictable things will happen in the classroom. This can be such things as the way class starts, daily warm-up activities, assignments written in the same place, daily reminders and routines, materials in the same places, or resources available as they expect.

Attention to social skills—Top priority is given to the teaching and practicing of social skills. The teacher does not assume that students automatically know appropriate interpersonal behavior.

Respect—It is the cornerstone of classroom life. The teacher treats all students with the same level of respect and teaches the students to do the same.

A reliable, consistent teacher—Students can trust the teacher to be an adult. They can count on the teacher to be fair, firm, and kind. They can be sure the teacher will listen to them. They can rely on the teacher to follow and reinforce agreed-upon and previously stated procedures and behaviors. They can be confident in the teacher's equitable responses. Consistency equals security. (Yes, even adolescents crave consistency. In some cases, teachers are the most stable things in a student's life. Okay, I admit that might be scary that we are the most stable things!)

Engaging learning activities—The academic life of the classroom is lively, fascinating, and geared to students' developmental needs. Lessons include variety, movement, differentiation, humor, technology, relevance, challenge, collaboration, and student choice. The teacher does not do all the talking. Students participate actively. Learning activities are divided into appropriate time segments. The teacher is always aware of the students' attention levels.

Tolerance for normal, useful disorder—The teacher recognizes the inattention, noise, and excitement necessary to the learning activity and appropriate to the age level. The atmosphere is not one of rigid control but is one that allows for "productive chaos." (Remember my opinions in Chapter 1 about how the madness is, in part, wonderful?)

Clear expectations—Protocols (ways of behaving and doing things) are thoughtfully designed, well explained, and clear to all members of the classroom. They have been put into writing—readily visible and available to students. The teacher models the protocols consistently.

Predictable consequences—Consequences are just as clear and consistent as expectations. Students know ahead of time what behaviors are not okay and what will happen if those behaviors show up.

Student contributions to codes of behavior—Students work with the teacher as a team to form classroom procedures, protocols, and consequences. They discuss respect, disrespect, and how they want to be treated (perhaps creating a "Bill of Rights" for the classroom). They discuss what procedures work best for classroom life.

Trusting partnerships with parents—The teacher is keenly aware of the significant role parents play in supporting classroom management strategies. Strong processes are in place for two-way communication, for keeping parents informed of all classroom expectations and events, for keeping regular contact with families about each individual student, and for communicating frequent compliments to support each student. Parents know the teacher is on their child's side. All contacts with the parents are positive and respectful.

Student organization—Students have tools and training for keeping track of their materials and assignments, for planning and completing their work, and for managing their schedules. The teacher does not assume that students automatically have good organizational skills, but teaches and reinforces these skills. Organizational routines and systems give students continuity, consistency, and better chances for success.

Teacher preparation—The teacher is ready for all the activities of the class or day. He or she is organized and prepared for each lesson from beginning to end. All supplies for lessons are gathered and in place. Activities have been tested beforehand. The teacher is calm, enthusiastic, and ready to welcome students at the door. This gives students the message that the teacher is ready for them, that the teacher has a plan for the class, and that learning begins when they arrive. This is reassuring for students. It also avoids all kinds of possible disruptions and delays.

Smooth transitions—Transitions between activities are anticipated, planned, and practiced. The teacher uses a variety of tactics for transitions. Sometimes the teacher makes a video of the instructions; any student who can't remember what to do can replay the video. Other times, music is used. Students must be moved and ready for the next task by the time the music ends. Sometimes small groups move one at a time. The teacher makes it fun. ("Anyone with a piercing may now move.") Sometimes there is a timed, no-talk move. (The timer is set, but anyone who talks has to start over on the move.) Students are always given advance warning of transitions so they can tidy up and collect supplies for the next activity.

Student voice and power—Students' suggestions, opinions, ideas, and reflections are welcomed. Students take an active role in planning learning experiences, management procedures, and other classroom events. As a group, they discuss individual and class needs. Students take part in working out solutions to problems that arise in the classroom.

Flexibility—While the teacher takes the already-stated consequences seriously, he or she also deals with each behavior problem on a case-by-case basis. Aware of individual needs and sensibilities, the teacher has a number of techniques for use with different students and different situations. While the classroom activities are well planned and students can expect the teacher to know where things are headed, neither the teacher nor the plan is rigid. When the needs of the students or some unforeseen event dictates, the teacher can change courses in a lesson plan to avert disaster or disconnection, or to grasp a teachable moment. This teacher has probably read the words of Albert Cullum's book *The Geranium on the Windowsill Just Died But Teacher You Went Right On*:

> The robins sang and sang and sang
> but teacher you went right on.
> The last bell sounded the end of the day
> but teacher you went right on.
> The geranium on the windowsill just died
> but teacher you went right on. (2000, p. 56)

Recovering Attention

Even during the most captivating of learning experiences, student attention can wander from the topic or task at hand. Sometimes the excitement of an experiment or investigation just carries them away! Some of the timeworn strategies for recapturing attention and refocusing work have become habits that we keep, even if they don't work. For example, have you ever said, "I will never do ____ in my classroom" but then find yourself doing that very thing (such as the following)?

- Saying "Shhh." "Shushing" is one of the worst management strategies, yet many of us do it daily. Do you know that if you make the noise long enough, you will run out of air and pass out? And of course, as your unconscious body hits the ground, the kids are thinking: "Free day!"

- Ignoring the behavior. Many times, we choose to just ignore inappropriate behavior in hopes that the student will stop. In numerous cases, minor annoying behaviors should be ignored (you can't react to every burp). But if it is something that has been specifically named as unacceptable, you have to respond. Let's say that there is a behavior with a well-stated consequence and you've given one warning, but the student repeats the act. If you ignore the behavior, you send a clear message to the whole class that you don't follow through with consequences. Every time you fail to follow through, your management weakens. This sets you up for many discipline struggles to come.

- Flicking the lights. Although this strategy might still work in some cases (maybe in kindergarten), if you do it more than ten times, the students think there's a disco ball and start to dance.

> Truly, it's okay to be a little nuts around your young adolescent students now and then. It can really help with classroom management.

Try these instead: These proactive ideas can replace some of your not-so-effective strategies. Some of them take high self-esteem on your part and a certain comfort level with the use of humor. With the first few, your students might run out of class seeking professional help for you. (But, maybe that is not a bad thing!)

- Have a conversation with the board (whiteboard or dry erase board—or could it be that you still have a chalkboard?). The next time you have trouble getting students to pay attention, walk over to the board and say, "Oh chalkboard, you will listen to me. You're the reason I became a teacher. I love you chalkboard . . ." (You could even start singing: "I love you chalkboard, oh, yes I do.") Students will say to each other, "Is he talking to the board? Shh! It must be important." When a teacher talks to an inanimate object, students listen.

- Stand on a chair and recite poetry. Be dramatic.

- Speak with words that don't make sense. Just start talking gibberish. Talk as though you are from a foreign country—or even better, another planet.

- When the group is off task, it's difficult to identify just one student causing the distraction in a group. So ordinarily you end up singling out the last student you noticed talking about something other than the work. It goes down like this: "Bernice, enough is enough! Please get back to work." Bernice defends herself (and rightly so): "Mr. Berckemeyer, everyone else in the group was talking just as much as I was, and you yelled at me and not the other kids!"

Next time—reprimand a student who is not in the room (a student who actually is not even a member of the class). "Bob, don't pretend I can't see you. Bob, I am so on the edge right now."

Meanwhile, your students will be thinking, "Who's Bob, and why is he in trouble?" (There is nothing wrong with being emotionally unstable around young adolescents. Go ahead and act like you could snap at any time. Don't worry; they've got your back. They'll go for help!)

- Stop talking. Or at least, stop using your vocal chords. Just talk, wave your arms—but make no sound. When they're quiet, you can resume talking. Or, you can give them time to talk. Tell them, "You have 30 seconds to say whatever is most important that you needed to say." Count down the last five seconds loudly.

- Instead of shushing students, face the class and take a deep breath (exaggerate the sound) and let it out. Do this a few times. They will start to notice. Ask them to join you. Have them do this several times in hopes that they will relax and quiet themselves. (Be on the alert for hyperventilation!)

- Develop some other consistent cue, clue, or gesture to reclaim attention of the group. You could even start singing or twitching!

- Be entertaining. Classrooms should be fun.

- If you use humor often in the classroom, students might have trouble telling if you are joking or being serious when you're trying to recover focus on the lesson. Ahead of time, establish a signal to communicate the difference. Teach them that you'll use a signal or a phrase such as saying (perhaps with hands across chest), "I am serious as a heart attack; you need to simmer down," or "I'm dead serious now." Giving them a prearranged cue will help them draw the line between class fun time and class focus time.

- If you need to get attention focused back on a lesson in progress, make a paper megaphone. Hold it to your mouth and loudly say, "Whiteboards up!" Hold one of their student dry erase boards up. Students will gradually figure out to grab theirs and mimic you, holding these above their heads. Then ask a question related to the topic of the lesson and give them 30 seconds to write an answer or a question mark (meaning they don't know). This gets their minds back to the lesson and allows you to find out if they understand what they've heard or seen so far in the lesson.

- Whole-class restlessness and inattention should alert you that the class needs a brain break or body stretch. Add some action to the lesson. Or, take a break: stop and show a short video clip, share three very good short jokes, or hold a two-minute dance party. Then get back to a task or switch to another activity to strengthen the same content, process, or skill.

Managing Disruptions and Misbehaviors

Ultimately, the goal of behavior management is to help students learn to manage their own behavior. So your interventions must allow the student to correct the misbehavior with as little fuss as possible. The more overt (dramatic) or teacher-centered (as opposed to student self-managed) the intervention, the more sensitive and defensive the student will feel, and the more learning time will be lost.

Use proactive in-class strategies that avert or minimize disruption to the learning process while avoiding struggles and helping students control themselves.

Follow the "Law of Least Intervention" for off-task, mildly distracting, or about-to-be distracting behaviors. (This strategy might also be called: "Become a pro at redirection.") Do this by constantly moving among students and observing who's engaged and who's disengaged. Make eye contact with kids who need it. Give a visual signal to a student who needs a nudge. Pause by a desk, place a hand on the student's desk, or just move near to a student. Point to the paper or other work materials. Give a soft reminder of the job. Don't walk away too quickly. Stay long enough to see that the behavior has changed.

Pay attention to whether a student might need a break ("Why don't you get a drink, Sam?"), a change of pace ("Do the first three problems, then give me a signal"), or a change of place ("Alana, I think you could work better over on the carpet").

If you have fairly consistent proactive management strategies, most of the disruptions will be minor and can be minimized or averted. But there are times when a behavior interferes with learning for others, challenges you, disrespects another student, or blatantly breaks some other clearly-taught rule. In these cases, you must intervene more actively. When you do, follow these guidelines:

- As best you can, remove the disruptive student from an audience.

- Address the issue as quickly as is possible.

- Speak to the student in private—away from others. When the student has an audience, he or she will have to save face so your efforts will go nowhere. Furthermore, it is important to preserve the student's dignity in the eyes of peers.

- Keep your emotions under control. Speak kindly and respectfully, but straightforwardly and honestly.

- Speak about the behavior, not the person. By focusing on the behavior, the chances for cooperation increase and the chances for defensiveness decrease. Don't bring up past misbehaviors. Focus only on this incident.

- Do not argue with the student.

- Honor the student's feelings. Make sure students know that they have a right to their feelings. Part of what you are doing is helping them to manage their behaviors to meet classroom expectations even when they are frustrated or angry.

- Keep your talk brief. Talking too much can lead to a power struggle. State the behavior. Remind the student of the appropriate behavior, stated in positive terms. For example, "In this class, we respect the privacy of each other's belongings". Then send the student back to work or redirect her or him to something else.

- Give the student the opportunity to resolve this quickly by getting control of his or her own behavior. The student can choose to do this or take the consequences. Consequences must be specific and proportional to the offensive behavior.

- If there is a consequence to be given and the student knew about it beforehand, apply the consequence. Then be done with it. The student should know that the consequence has been assigned and this incident is over. Make a clean sweep of it!

- Help the student return to the classroom with dignity. Make sure there are no comments made to or about her or him by other students.

- Perhaps the behavior was precipitated by the student's confusion about the content or inability to do a task. Be sure you are tuned in to this. If this has a failure beneath the issue, do what it takes to help the student feel successful with the task.

Managing Escalating Misbehaviors

Owning up to misbehavior in front of peers is very difficult for young adolescents. It's the last thing they want to do. Rather than taking ownership or responsibility for their actions, they find it easier to blame other students or the teacher.

Here's a typical classroom situation: Realizing she has forgotten the homework assignment, a student comes out with, "Mr. Toombs, this class is stupid, and you wore the same pants three days in a row." (Isn't it interesting how young adolescents can remember your weekly clothing choices but cannot remember yesterday's homework assignment?)

When situations escalate to open hostility, blaming, or disrespect, some emotional buttons might get pushed (yours!). No matter what your level of frustration, maintain your poise and be very respectful to the student. Take care not to respond in any way that would belittle, ridicule, or embarrass the student. Do not use any sarcasm. Any aggressive behavior on your part makes the student feel cornered. Constantly worried about how they are and will be perceived by others in the room, young adolescents find that the easiest target of all is the teacher. They know how to exploit our biggest flaws. The other students take notice and find it humorous, thus providing the student with needed attention, power, and a diversion from their behavior.

Example: Watch how a simple classroom incident, handled reactively, can escalate during one school day: Kurt comes to his first-period class with no homework for the fifth time in a row. Having had enough, the teacher points out that not doing his homework is affecting his success in this class. His classmates hear the teacher's judgment as "Kurt, I am tired of this lazy behavior" or "I am sick of reminding you constantly about doing your work" or "You're a poor student." Essentially, the teacher has embarrassed Kurt and taken away his power. Kurt already has deep struggles with being accepted by his peers. These skyrocket. Worse, he fears that peers will now see him as weaker and will find ways to further threaten his power.

During a second-period cooperative learning activity, students in the group to which Kurt is assigned let him know that they don't want him in the group because his laziness won't help them get a good grade. Already, the incident with the first-period teacher is lessening his power. In third-period class, Kurt sees a way to get his power back. He finds a weaker student and pounces on that student like a tiger on fresh kill.

The teacher observes this and reprimands Kurt: "Stop that! You need to stop picking on other students." And the loss of power continues.

Later in the hallway when the first-period teacher sees Kurt pushing a younger student, she speaks up (in front of other students), "Kurt, that is enough. You have not been doing your work, and now you are bullying other kids." Off to the office goes Kurt. Now he feels completely powerless, and doubles down on his goal to get power back by any means. What the first teacher thought was an appropriate response to Kurt's homework issue (but was actually an over-use of adult power in reactive rather than proactive ways) escalated a misdeed into a serious problem for the student.

As teachers, we have little time to reflect on such situations that occur in our classes. We react and move on. We are busy and trying to do the best we can. But we must remember that our students spend many hours in fear—fear of their peers, parents, and teachers. We can plan ahead for these occurrences with students and be ready to respond in ways that reverse or halt the escalation.

- Don't start by confronting the student in front of others. When we do this, we reinforce a message and set an example for other students. Always stop and ask: "What will my response do to the student? And what will the other students hear in my response?" As with less volatile situations, take the time to talk to your student alone before or after class.

- If a student is belligerent or uncooperative, back off for a few moments. Offer a hall pass to the student, suggest getting a drink of water, or encourage the student to go to the restroom and splash some water on his or her face. Ask her to be back in seven minutes (or other reasonable time limit). Send him on an errand to deliver something to another class. Give her a spot in the room to write in a journal or draw her feelings.

- Before you make the choice to send the student off to the office with a behavior referral, set a time for a talk. Usually, when offered a choice to talk about an escalating issue (as an alternative to being sent off to the office), the student will accept, and the two of you can get to the bottom of it. Be patient. Let the student talk. Listen. Really listen. Be fair and caring. Ask gentle, nonjudgmental questions that help them explore their issues, fears, hopes, and worries.

- When you talk with students, be clear about their options. If they've persisted in a behavior that is not acceptable, be firm and clear about what the consequence will be and why. (Actually, they should already know what the consequence will be.) But lay out a way they can complete whatever is needed to meet the consequence. Help them build courage to tackle the problem.

- Find a way to address the details of the incident. For example, if it's about forgotten homework assignments, come up with a way for the student to succeed at remembering the assignment. Suggest some new tools. Send a text so she has it on her phone. If it's about not bringing materials, find out why. Maybe his family doesn't have enough money for notebooks and pencils. Find a way to get the supplies needed. If work isn't complete, keep the student after class and monitor him finishing the work. Talk with team members or other teachers about the whole picture of the student. Make a phone call home to enlist help from the parents. Do all these things before grabbing the behavior referral form. These strategies would have been better ways for the teacher to respond to Jacob back in the example at the beginning of the chapter.

- Track down other teachers who have this student in class and explain what kind of day the student is having. Other teachers can look out for that student and her interactions with other students and perhaps ward off escalation of the issue.

- After talking to a student, don't expose any of the personal matters—ever. Keep students' confidences. When they trust you with information, don't share it, even with other teachers. (There are legal exceptions to this.)

- Follow up your talk by checking in with the student the next day and on future days. Listen to what's happening and how the student is feeling about it. Continue to do what you can to boost the student's belief that he or she can change the behavior or solve the problem. If you've contacted parents as a part of this process, follow up with them too.

- Plan ways to empower all the students in your classroom. In particular, when a student is having a rough day and you've had to confront any sort of issue, invite the student to help you with something. This can form a relationship bridge with the student. Any class engagement instills power in kids. Assign responsibilities to students who tend to bully; this will give them legitimate, constructive ways to use their power.

- Whenever there is any kind of a private conversation with a student about a behavior issue (be it social or academic behavior)—whether or not it involves a referral—operate with the attitude that every day is a new day. Let students know that you give them a new start each day and that you want them to see each day as a chance for a fresh start. This is the great thing about addressing problems right away, dealing with them, and taking care of the already-clarified consequences. It's done quickly. And when it is, students don't have to drag the shame around with them for days. They get a fresh start.

Example: Here's how a teacher handled an escalating problem proactively: The teacher was astonished when a student responded to an assignment in math class with "Ms. Fante, this is stupid. I hate this class" (accompanied by a lot of eye rolling and evil looks). Ordinarily, Marina was a cooperative student; she had not been disrespectful like this before. When the behavior repeated itself for several days, the teacher became hurt and angered at the hostility.

Resisting the instinct to send Marina to the office with a write-up for not doing her work and being so disrespectful, Ms. Fante asked Marina to stay after class. She did write a referral. Placing it in front of the student, Ms. Fante voiced her confusion about the sudden change in attitude. She asked Marina to read the referral. Then she asked her to decide if she wanted the form to be sent to the office or if she wanted to talk about the problem.

After an initial (and typical) response of "I don't care!" and a few minutes of silence, Marina started talking. "Ms. Fante, I have been having such a bad week. My friends have been making fun of me and saying I did something I did not do. They are spreading horrible rumors about me." Asking gentle questions, Ms. Fante talked with Marina for a long time about this underlying issue. She promised that she would work with Marina to solve this. Like all great teachers at this level, Ms. Fante knew that without working on the social and emotional needs of a young adolescent, she could never successfully address the academic needs. Then she asked Marina to make a plan for changing her class conduct and catching up on the work she had refused to do.

A Few Words About Referrals

When conflict arises in the classroom, teachers tend to want to throw the responsible student(s) out of the classroom. "Let the office deal with her!" they think. However, when we send a student to the office, we lose some of our power. How many times have we said to a student, "I am sending you to the office, and when you get back, I will also be talking to you about a consequence"?

Time and time again, teachers say, "I sent her to the office, and they did nothing." Here's an observation of mine: Administrators will never be as mad as you are. No matter how many times you underline or how many words you bold on the referral form, an administrator will not be as emotional as you are.

First piece of advice: Never write the referral in the heat of passion. Teachers have been known to write a referral with 23 exclamation marks on the form.

Second piece of advice: Watch what you say on the referral form. Once I wrote on a referral, "I am so sick, I am sick, sick, sick." My principal (who had a great sense of humor) wrote back on the form, "You are also redundant." Compared to some referrals sent to the office, this one was mild. Just ask any administrator to see his or her file of classic referrals submitted by irrational teachers.

Third piece of advice: When referring a student to the office for using inappropriate language, just leave it at "inappropriate language; call me for details." During a phone call with a parent, you can then mention the word if they ask for it, or you can tell your administrator.

Fourth piece of advice: When you prepare to talk to parents as a part of the process related to a referral (or any other time you talk to parents about a behavior problem), do not plan on them having an "aha" moment. Parents tend to know if their child is unorganized, because they see the kid's room every day. Parents see their child's disrespectful attitude toward others, and they even know if their child is late, unmotivated, or unprepared. Although they might not want to admit to these issues, there's a good chance that parents do know they exist.

Fifth piece of advice: Take time to follow up with the student after a referral. You can use this as a teachable moment to help a student plan for a different action when such a situation occurs in the future. Remember: If you throw a kid out 30 times, he comes back 31 times (unless he moves). So work hard to keep or rebuild a good relationship with that student.

Last piece of advice (repetitive from earlier in the chapter): Always talk to a student before making a referral. Yes, it takes time, patience, and effort to talk with the student about what is happening in his or her life. Yes, it takes time to do the follow-up. However, the bottom line is that just sending the student to the office does nothing for you and possibly nothing for the student. It does not improve your relationship with the student; it does not increase the student's trust in you and other adults. Give a good hearty try to resolve the issue with the student before turning her or him over to someone else. This does not mean that you should not seek input from other adults in the school. To intervene in ways that are most beneficial for the student, there will be times when all the adults who care about the student will need to get together. But as a matter of habit, for routine (even tough or annoying) classroom behaviors, talk to the student first!

Interventions and Shared Discipline

When a student has a recurring issue that affects behavior or academic progress and performance, there is need for adult response beyond or in addition to the usual classroom management procedures and school referral procedures. This should come in the form of an intervention that includes all the people concerned with the student's welfare: the student, the teacher(s), the school counselor, and the parents. See Chapter 7 for some suggestions about creating a team (or other group) intervention process for students who need it.

Ending the Class

Proactive management doesn't end when kids pack up to leave the class. It doesn't end until students have left the school grounds for the day. Don't finish your class in chaos with students running out the door. Never let students leave the room until you have dismissed them.

Yes, this practice gives you a chance for them to gather up their stuff (not leave it for you to deal with) and tidy up the room. Yes, this gives you and the next class a chance for some order. But the primary reason for an orderly dismissal is that it ends class on a congenial, positive note for everyone. You want students to leave feeling cared for. You want to maintain the relationships every minute they are inside that room. So choose a favorite farewell phrase to send them off. Say it as their signal to leave. Use the perky, fun goodbye phrase every day—no exceptions! Then stand at the door and have a last moment of contact with each student with such send-offs as:

"Have a nice day!"

"Ciao, bambinos!"

"Yes, I will miss you."

"Later, alligators!"

"Thanks for your hard work today."

"Hasta la vista, baby!"

"Have a good one!"

"See you later!"

"The room looks good! So long!"

"Thanks, and I appreciate your spirit today!"

"Thanks, and be safe out there."

"Get out!" (not a good choice, but sometimes you might be thinking it!)

In addition to the goodbye phrase, you could also dismiss the class by groups such as students wearing blue, those with black tennis shoes, those with hazel eyes, or those with first names that begin with a certain letter. Mix it up and be creative. You can also offer friendly reminders while they wait to be released: "Don't forget to check your assignment book and the assignment board, and bring in your moldy science project."

Here's another idea: Every once in a while, pick a student to do the dismissal. It gives students power and is a great way to involve them.

Final Note: Young adolescents want to be secure and respected. They like a teacher who is a little strict and has good classroom management skills. Their lives are filled with change, uncertainty, and often with inconsistency. They are comforted by your consistency. They admire and may even emulate (secretly) the respect and other behaviors you model. We teachers are there for them unconditionally—every day. We wait for them; we greet them; we provide a safe environment for them; and we send them off with cheer and hope. They need this. They deserve this!

For Reflection and Action

1. List a few elements of proactive management from this chapter that you would like to try or improve upon. Set some goals for yourself. In two weeks, reflect on what you did and how it worked.

2. Think about a behavior problem you have recently handled. What did you do? What elements were reactive? What elements were proactive? How did the student(s) respond?

3. Choose the problem you identified in #2 or another incident during which you wish you had responded differently. Write down the problem. Plan a proactive solution or response that you will use the next time a similar situation arises.

4. For three days, keep a record of student behavior incidents that led to a talk with the student or the application of a consequence. Reflect on how you might have averted or diminished any of the problems before they got to the point of a private talk, consequence, or referral.

5. For the above list, reflect on your follow up. How soon did you follow up? How did you follow up? What did you learn from the follow up? If you did not follow up, consider what barriers kept you from doing so. With a colleague, discuss possible solutions to the barriers.

Source: *Managing the Madness: A Practical Guide to Understanding Young Adolescents and Classroom Management*
© Association for Middle Level Education   www.amle.org

CHAPTER 7

Intervention That Works

Mr. Berckemeyer, send me to the office. They are nicer to me there.

What happens when a student's behavior or academic problems persist and are not satisfactorily alleviated by the system of protocols, procedures, and consequences practiced in the individual classroom? What happens when a particular incident is so alarming that the classroom teacher struggles to address it with his or her usual responses? On these questions, I'd side with an approach that gives teachers or teams the power to issue major consequences (such as suspensions or detention) or design other "big" interventions. This may seem radical to those who hold to a common approach that places the "major issues" in the hands of administrators. When an adolescent says, "They suspended me," that student views the office personnel, dean of students, assistant principal, or principal as the primary disciplinarian. The office—not the teacher—is the enforcer.

When teachers reclaim their power and take ownership of managing their students (as opposed to always passing off the hard stuff to "the office"),

- The teacher decides and communicates consequences for behavior.
- The teacher facilitates the follow-through with the student.
- The teacher communicates with the student and family or caretakers involved.
- The students view the teacher as the main person at the school confronting and helping her or him with behavior or academic issues.
- The teacher controls and handles student make-up work or missing assignments.
- The teacher can involve the student, parents, and administrators in figuring out how best to help the student.

- There is more discussion about student behavior or specific academic needs.

- The teacher becomes the student's advocate.

- The student-teacher relationship is deepened.

- The teacher is empowered.

Please note: It's understood here that laws or school policies require administrators to handle the course of certain offenses. This may include such things as fighting or other forms of violence including some bullying acts; certain uses of inappropriate language; vandalism; carrying weapons; skipping school; or use or possession of drugs, tobacco, or alcohol.

When the "office" holds the power to handle all "the big problems," the teacher's power is diminished. When I am Ruler of Education, students will see their teachers as the primary managers, problem-solvers, and disciplinarians.

Shared Interventions and Discipline

There are times when the best course for a teacher is to enlist outside help, when, for the best interest of a student (and yourself), your classroom management must involve adults beyond your classroom. This happens for a variety of reasons, and not all of them are about dire or out-of-control situations. Many of the reasons have to do with putting more heads together to enable a student to make headway in taking control and responsibility for civil or productive behavior. *Any time* a student needs targeted help (beyond what is working well in the classroom) to practice appropriate behavior or to address a persistent academic need is *the right time* for an intervention that includes a larger group.

In great middle schools and high schools, teachers and administrators work together to solve problems related to serious student needs. *However, what is critical in this process is that the teacher or the team must be the ones to initiate the intervention process and follow through with the consequences and the plan for improvement.*

This is not an easy task. It takes time and trust to keep this much of the power management in the hands of teachers. Let's be honest, sometimes we teachers are not the most rational people when dealing with troublesome students. After all, we are often the ones directly involved with their acting out. Admittedly, teachers might over-react on occasion. There are situations for which (in the teacher's mind) a ten-week suspension seems logical—even if there are only five weeks of school remaining. (You might think the student's future teaching team owes you, since the student's sentence will run through the first five weeks of next school year!)

Because persistent issues are exasperating, none of us is rational all the time. It's a good thing, then, when all the adults—teams, teachers, administrators, and parents concerned with the student join together to solve a problem.

A Five-Step Plan

I suggest the following approach for teachers, teams, and administrators to share ownership of management issues, when needed. It's intended and workable for behavioral issues or academic needs. The plan I share here uses the model of a school with a teaming structure. If your school is not team-based, assume that your "team" includes teachers and other adults in the school who work with the student. The plan includes these steps:

      Step 1: Describe and document.

      Step 2: Create goals and strategies (as a team or other teacher group).

      Step 3: Bring the student into the meeting and make a plan.

      Step 4: Inform and involve parents and administrators.

      Step 5: Follow through and follow up.

Note: The verb *document* will show up many times in the explanation of the steps. Don't forget to keep a record of what happens at all phases of the process. Begin by having a completed form, such as the one in Figure 7-1, and adapt this to your own needs.) Keep this in a place where any of the teachers involved can access it easily. Keeping this handy enables the teacher to make a necessary call before an issue becomes ancient history and the student has moved on to further incidents.

Figure 7-1 *Student's Home Contact Information*

_____ Team _____ Year

Student _____

Homeroom _____

Parent or Guardian name(s) _____

Other Contacts:

Contact #1

Name _____

Relationship_____ Phone _____

Email _____

Address _____

Contact #2

Name _____

Relationship_____ Phone _____

Email _____

Address _____

Contact #3

Name _____

Relationship_____ Phone _____

Email _____

Address _____

The teacher or team needs to be aware of:

_____

_____

Source: *Managing the Madness: A Practical Guide to Understanding Young Adolescents and Classroom Management*
© Association for Middle Level Education   www.amle.org

Step 1 Describe and document the issue.

Any time a group of adults meets to collaborate on a plan for a student, the main teacher involved must meet three prerequisites:

1) Describe in writing the concern to be addressed.

2) Inform the student's parents (or guardians) and the appropriate administrator about the issue and about the meeting.

3) Document all communications and actions to date related to the issue and meeting(s).

Describe (teacher): The teacher who has first-hand contact with the problem briefly describes the issue and the reason for the meeting. Keep academic and behavioral issues separate. Address them in separate meetings.

The reason for an academic intervention might be such an issue as:

- Repeatedly not completing work
- Repeatedly not doing work at all
- Too much time diverted from learning activities
- Repeatedly late assignments
- Lack of engagement or participation in class
- Missing considerable class work due to absences
- Missing homework

The reason for a behavioral intervention might be such an issue as:

- Repeatedly bothering others
- Disrespecting the teacher or others
- Repeatedly coming to class without materials
- Bullying
- Roaming during class
- Disrupting class
- Using inappropriate humor or language

In addition to knowing about the issue, all attendees at the meeting need to see a record of previous communication regarding the situation. Use a form such as the "Intervention Communication Log" (Figure 7-2) to describe the issue and the communication that has occurred about the matter.

Figure 7-2 *Intervention Communication Log*

_____ Team _____ Year

Student _____ Teacher _____

Reason or issue: _____

_____

Communication: _____

_____

_____ Phone call   Date: _____   Spoke to: _____

_____ Letter sent   Date: _____   Spoke to: _____

_____ Email sent   Date: _____   Spoke to: _____

_____ Meeting scheduled   Date: _____

Other communications regarding this issue: _____

What?   **When?**   **Who?**

_____   Date: _____   Persons involved: _____

_____   Date: _____   Persons involved: _____

Results of communication: _____

_____

Action planned, who is responsible for what, and target date: _____

_____

Follow-up communications regarding this issue:

What?   **When?**   **Who?**

_____   Date: _____   Persons involved: _____

_____   Date: _____   Persons involved: _____

Source: *Managing the Madness: A Practical Guide to Understanding Young Adolescents and Classroom Management*
© Association for Middle Level Education   www.amle.org

Describe (student): Before a meeting, the student involved should also be given an opportunity to reflect on and describe the matter. This should happen as soon as possible after an incident or issue is identified as being in need of more attention. Give the student an appropriate amount of time (at school) to complete a "Student Academic Reflection" form (for an academic issue) or a "Student Behavior Reflection" form (for a behavior issue). See Figures 7-3 and 7-4. Adapt these as needed for your students. The teacher giving the sheet to the student should collect it from him or her and make an extra copy.

Inform: I'm quite sure that any educator receiving an administrative certificate is simultaneously awarded a special chip implant in his or her brain. Forever after, when a teacher says, "I'm having a problem with ____(student name)," the chip is activated and the administrator automatically responds, "Did you call the parent?"

Calling the parent is the first line of defense. Hopefully, you have already established powerful connections with your students' parents or guardians—with ongoing information and communication that affirms each student and family. If so, when a problem such as this one arises, the parents already believe you are on their child's side and you will already have discussed the child's strengths, challenges, needs, and progress.

If you have not already discussed this particular matter with the parents, contact them now. Let them know about the issue (including what has already been tried), the meeting, the reason for the meeting, the timing of the meeting, and who will be there. Get input from the parents that you or they think would be helpful. Assure the parents that you'll stay in communication with them on this matter. It is not always necessary for a parent or guardian to be a part of a meeting with a student. However, if the parent's presence is needed, use this call to invite him (or her or them) to the meeting. By the way, don't use a text message, email, or phone message for this information. Talk directly to the parent. Do confirm the meeting or matter discussed with a mailed letter or email.

Document: Have you ever had a call to a parent about misbehavior backfire?

"Ms. Clark, this is Mr. Berckemeyer calling from Scott Carpenter Middle School about your daughter Olivia. Yesterday she used some inappropriate language with me and became a little violent."

The parent responds, "Oh, Mr. Berckemeyer, I am glad you called. Olivia comes home every night crying because you are picking on her."

Figure 7-3 *Student Academic Reflection*

_____ Team _____ Year

Student _____ Date _____

1. Describe the situation or problem:

_____

_____

2. How did your behavior help or hurt the situation?

_____

_____

3. If you had a chance to do it all over again, what would you do differently?

_____

_____

4. What goals will you set for improving this?

_____

_____

5. What ideas do you have to make sure this situation changes for the better?

_____

_____

NOTES

Consequences given: _____

Goals set: _____

Plans or strategies: _____

Additional comments: _____

Signatures

Teacher _____ Student _____

Source: *Managing the Madness: A Practical Guide to Understanding Young Adolescents and Classroom Management*
© Association for Middle Level Education   www.amle.org

Suddenly, you are the one in trouble, and then you backpedal, saying, "I will talk to her about these issues."

The parent replies, "Good, because if you don't, I will call the principal. Besides, she gets along with all her other teachers!"

After you've made contact with the parent, add the details to the log of communications on the issue. When teachers and teams keep records of calls, meetings, emails, and other conversations related to a student's needs, they build a history of a student's academic and behavioral growth. Keep the log in a notebook or, even better, create a file for every student and put the communication log in each file.

Step 2 Create goals and strategies (as a team or other teacher group).

Teachers' lounge discussions and team meetings can become unproductive venting sessions that accomplish nothing. How many times have you walked out of a team meeting and said, "That was the biggest waste of time"? Either the team focused too much time on one student, or there was no resolution to the problem.

Here's a rule that I promote for team meetings wherein teachers are dealing with student issues: *The team gets three free vents about a particular student.* After the student's behaviors or academic actions (or lack thereof) have been vented, it's time for the teachers to move to solutions.

In planning the meeting, the teacher initiating the intervention must decide who needs to be at the meeting. This should include any teachers regularly involved with the student. It might also include an administrator, a counselor, and parents. (There may be a follow-up meeting where parents can be involved if they're not needed at the beginning.)

For this step of the plan, teachers will have already reviewed the "Intervention Communication Log" (Figure 7-2) that describes the issue and the communications to date on the matter. In a meeting, teachers identify *one to three specific goals* they'd like to see the student meet. Resist the urge to create a list of 50 things you want changed by tomorrow. Remember: The student is a young adolescent who, by definition, has only been alive for 10 to 15 years. Mistakes will be made; authority will be challenged; "what the big deal is" will be a mystery to the student. So focus on no more than three things. In many cases, one or two goals are plenty. Hone in on the most important issue. And this is critical: do not mix academic issues with behavior issues. There are connections between the two, of course. But it's difficult for young adolescents to make those connections. Just be assured that improvement in academic areas will positively affect behavior and vice versa.

Next, the teachers choose *three to five strategies for solving the problem*. These are strategies to be followed by the teacher(s), student, or parent(s), or a mixture thereof. This process will certainly involve brainstorming and discussion of a number of possible strategies and approaches. (See Figures 7-5 and 7-6 for some intervention strategy ideas. These forms can also be used later when you make a plan with the student.)

Teachers in the meeting should also agree on who will be responsible for taking each action. Keep in mind that when the student joins the meeting, he or she may suggest other ideas. In the process of reflecting on and describing the situation, the student will have thought about actions or consequences for changing the situation in the future. So your planned strategies may change.

Also keep this in mind: Whatever brilliant strategies you devise, you'll have to implement them! If you don't find relevant, workable strategies, I guarantee you'll be talking about this same student and the same behaviors until the end of the school year. If the ideas fail or you don't follow through on them and go back to venting about that student, you must come up with and try three more ideas. This technique just might stop the complaining and result in a solution for the problem!

Step 3 Bring the student into the meeting and make a plan.

Empowered teachers involve students in every aspect of their daily school lives—and this definitely includes discussions about their behavioral or academic issues. Some students go from class to class causing misery and chaos or deep concern wherever they alight: a nervous breakdown for the first-period teacher, a popped blood vessel in the eyeball for the second-period teacher, and a relapse to smoking plus a new nervous tick for the third-period teacher. Needless to say, the student's fourth-period teacher will retire early, and she has only taught for four years!

This is a normal day for some young adolescents. If you happen to walk into the teachers' lounge and merely mention that student's name, one teacher passes out, one gets up to go smoke, and two others just sit there with dazed, confused looks on their faces. Meanwhile, the student is enjoying lunch, looking forward to the essentials classes coming up in the afternoon.

Figure 7-4 *Student Behavior Reflection*

_____ Team _____ Year

Student _____ Date _____

1. . Describe the situation that happened:

_____

_____

2. How did your behavior help or hurt the situation?

_____

_____

3. If you had a chance to do it all over again, what would you do differently?

_____

_____

4. What consequences should be given?

_____

_____

5. What ideas do you have to make sure this situation does not happen again?

_____

_____

NOTES

Consequences given: _____

Goals set: _____

Plans or strategies: _____

Additional comments: _____

Signatures

Teacher _____ Student _____

Source: *Managing the Madness: A Practical Guide to Understanding Young Adolescents and Classroom Management*
© Association for Middle Level Education   www.amle.org

Figure 7-5 *Academic Intervention Log*

Student _____ Homeroom _____ Date _____

Academic challenges observed by the team or teacher:

_____

_____

Classroom Teacher Intervention   **Team Member Responsible/
                                                       Date(s) Implemented**

- Conference with student   _____

- Sign agenda book before the student leaves class   _____

- Phone call with parent   _____

- Parent meeting at school with student and teachers _____

- Daily progress report given and sent home with student _____

- Use of a peer tutor   _____

- Modified assignment   _____

- Notes provided for the student   _____

- Have student repeat directions to the teacher   _____

- Weekly teacher assistance   _____

- Cleaning out notebook   _____

- Cleaning out locker or desk   _____

- Cleaning out backpack   _____

- Provide help at lunch or after school   _____

- Verbal checks for understanding   _____

- Use of advanced organizers   _____

- Plan of improvement created and follow-up assigned _____

- Provide an adult mentor   _____

- Team study hall recommended   _____

- Pace instruction differently for the student   _____

- Offer alternative assessment or assignment   _____

- Hold a child study meeting with counselors and
  other support staff   _____

Figure 7-5 *Academic Intervention Log* (continued)

Classroom Teacher Intervention	Team Member Responsible/ Date(s) Implemented
• Team discussion about student	_____
• Have student attend team meeting; establish goals and timeline with students	_____
• Other:	_____
Student Responsibilities	
• Fill out missing assignment sheet when work is not completed	_____
• Record homework and assignments in student agenda or planner	_____
• Attend help sessions at lunch or before or after school	_____
• Organize binder and notebook	_____
• Clean out locker or desk	_____
• Clean out backpack on a weekly basis	_____
• Seek help and support when needed	_____
• Start work and see what can be accomplished before asking for help	_____
• Ask another student for help or advice	_____
• Other:	_____
Parent Involvement	
• Provide tutoring	_____
• Check student planner or agenda nightly	_____
• Clean out backpack and notebooks	_____
• Meet with team	_____
• Conference call with team on a weekly basis	_____
• Set up study time at home	_____
• Call teachers when concerns arise	_____
• Set up monthly meeting with school counselor and support team	_____
• Other:	_____

Source: *Managing the Madness: A Practical Guide to Understanding Young Adolescents and Classroom Management*
© Association for Middle Level Education

Okay, so your teacher group has drafted some ideas (strategies, consequences, etc.) with little time wasted venting. Now it's time to bring the student to the group meeting. Go to the student's essentials (aka electives) classroom and ask if you can borrow him or her for a few minutes. Nine times out of ten, the essentials teacher will tell you to keep him or her for the entire hour. Sending a note saying the core team requires the presence of this student appears rude and disrespects the essentials teacher. Walking down to the room opens up communication and allows you to walk back with the student. You'd be amazed at how much you can accomplish by walking from the band room to the seventh grade hall with the student who will be attending the team meeting.

1. *Welcome the student.* Bring the student into a setting that is as comfortable as possible. Sit in a circle so the student doesn't feel diminished by position. You don't want the student to feel on trial. Inject warmth and even appropriate humor.

2. *Hear the student.* One teacher in the group is holding the reflection sheet that the student already completed for Step 1 of this process ("Academic Reflection" or "Behavior Reflection," Figure 7-3 or 7-4). Give the sheet to the student and ask him or her to share the reflections. This gives the security of presenting something she or he has already thought through. Especially important is the question asking how the student's behavior helped or hurt the situation or another person.

3. *Discuss ideas.* The student will have already suggested ideas on the reflection sheet. Honor these and do your best to incorporate them. The student's ideas provide a good starting point for a discussion that leads to setting goals, consequences, and plans and strategies for improvement. The teachers add their pre-discussed ideas.

It is critical that the young adolescent engage in the conversation about the behavior or academic performance and collaborate on decision-making about the next steps. This gives power to the student, lets the student know that the adults take his or her input seriously, and strengthens the trusting relationship between student and teachers. And ultimately, this involvement in the decisions increases the likelihood that the student will actually follow through on the plan. (And yes, the student must be held accountable for follow-through!)

4. *Make a plan.* As a group, set goals and identify strategies that will be followed by the student and by other parties. The "Academic Intervention Log" and "Behavior Intervention Log" (Figures 7-5 and 7-6) provide samples of the kinds of responses and strategies that the team might plan. Create such forms as these (adapted to your needs). A log of the intervention gives a plan in writing for all parties. It documents your decisions and follow-through efforts. Be clear with each other about who is to do what. Set clear dates and deadlines for actions.

5. *Review expectations and set rewards.* The meeting must not end until the student is clear about what will happen next. Make sure that agreements about what the student will do are provided to the student in writing. Review these verbally and have the student repeat them back.

With any intervention, it is important that consequences already stated for particular behaviors (academic or otherwise) be assigned. These include classroom rules or consequences and school-wide rules or consequences. In some cases there may need to be adaptations, but students must know that you take those pre-taught policies and consequences seriously.

You may also wish to establish a rewards system for the student. Set the expectations and the time frame. Then provide the student with a reward date. To avoid actually rewarding a student for something she was supposed to do in the first place, clarify that a reward is for working hard to change a habit or conquer a challenging problem. Young adolescents respond to many types of rewards; here are a few suggestions:

- A reward that the student selects—Students might ask for things you cannot provide or that are not fair, but knowing what motivates that child is good information.

- Time—Young adolescents love extra time for work, extra time between classes, time to talk with friends, or five minutes playing basketball with a friend or a teacher.

- Privileges—Choose an activity, responsibility, or task that the student has previously wanted or missed out on.

Figure 7-6 *Behavior Intervention Log*

Student _____ Homeroom _____ Date _____

Behavior issues observed by the team or teacher:

_____

_____

Classroom Teacher Intervention   **Team Member Responsible/
                                                       Date(s) Implemented**

• Preferred seating
  — Close to teacher   _____
  — Center of the room or front   _____

• Positive reinforcement for desired behaviors   _____

• Lunch detention   _____

• After school detention   _____

• Conference with student   _____

• Phone call to parent   _____

• Team meeting with student   _____

• Assign an adult mentor or student mentor   _____

• Referral   _____

• One-on-one meeting with student and a teacher   _____

• Meeting with support staff and counselor   _____

• Hold a child study meeting   _____

• Create a behavior contract   _____

• Suggest in-school suspension   _____

• Saturday school   _____

• Suggest out-of-school suspension   _____

• Establish rewards   _____

• Other: _____

Figure 7-6 *Behavior Intervention Log* (continued)

Student Responsibilities

**Team Member Responsible/
Date(s) Implemented**

- Communicate with teacher when angry or
frustrated before acting out

  _____

- Use a time-out area

  _____

- Use conflict resolution procedures

  _____

- Use a self-reminder system when acting out

  _____

- Isolate yourself when angry

  _____

- Talk to an adult when needing advice on
how to handle peers or other issues

  _____

- Self-monitor behavior contract

  _____

- Seek out positive reinforcement from
peers and teachers

  _____

- Stay consistent

  _____

- Other:

  _____

Parent Responsibility

- Communicate with teachers

  _____

- Attend team meetings

  _____

- Come to school with child

  _____

- Discuss issues with counselor or support staff

  _____

- Follow up with behavior contract

  _____

- Offer rewards

  _____

- Stay consistent

  _____

- Other:

  _____

Source: *Managing the Madness: A Practical Guide to Understanding Young Adolescents and Classroom Management*
© Association for Middle Level Education

www.amle.org

- Simple rewards such as snacks—Healthful snacks may not be the most popular, but many adolescents will eat almost anything.

- Attention from the teacher—Some students may want to spend time with a particular teacher at lunch (which might become a punishment for the teacher). However, spending the time with a student can make a world of difference to him or her.

Note: The best rewards involve time and interaction. In spite of the popularity of food and drinks as rewards, the bottom line is that many kids cause problems to get attention. Think of rewards that offer the most precious gift—your time.

Before the student leaves the meeting, be sure that all expectations, consequences, deadlines, and rewards are given to the student in writing. These can be written on the student's copy of the reflection sheet (Figure 7-3 or 7-4.) Or you can create a contract for the student with this information. Make enough copies of whatever signed agreement results from the meeting for all parties involved (including parents, administrators, teachers, and the student).

6. *Document everything.* Keep a clear record of the time a student spends in the meeting and of the meeting outcomes. Add to this record as you follow up after the meeting. Some schools do this documentation online for easy access by all team members and the guidance counselor. You and your team will need this information as you collaborate throughout the year with parents and administrators on the student's improvements.

Step 4: Inform and involve parents and administrators

After the student attends the team meeting, talk with your administrator and call the parents with the results of the meeting.

State clearly and concisely what goals and strategies were set. Let the parent know what the teachers will do, what the student will do, and what is needed for the parent to do.

In some cases, it will be helpful to schedule another meeting with the team, student, and parents to discuss specifics of the student's plan or to discuss outcomes after the plan is in place. If a meeting with parents is not warranted at this point, still provide parents with a written summary of the meeting (including goals and strategies for all parties) and a copy of the agreement with the student. Keep contact with the parents on this matter until it is successfully resolved. It never hurts to over-communicate. Make sure your documentation is current throughout the whole process.

> Part of teachers' taking on the ownership of discipline means dealing with communication issues that arise. Keep parents and administrators in the loop.

Step 5: Follow through and follow up.

The final, and essential, step is to follow up. Even if the student and parent leave the meeting with clearly defined responsibilities, it will be the teacher's job to hold people accountable. Each teacher on the team (or other group) must hold to his or her commitments.

As a part of holding students accountable, teachers must remind the students of their commitments to improve. If a student misses an obligation, here's what to do: As soon as the student arrives the next day, remind him or her of the expectations created during the meeting. For example, remind the student of the goal of "four good days or two good weeks of following the agreed-upon plan." (Keep the time goal short: none of this "Behave for the rest of your life" stuff.) Because adolescents need reminders, each teacher on the team should follow this procedure for several days. You might even need to bring the student back in for a "team talk." (Some students need one or two meetings. Others may need ten or more. You know your kids; you know what works.) Reminders are key. Yes, they take time, but we must hold young adolescents accountable.

Step up to support the student's improvement efforts. If the student makes a misstep, help him or her get back on track. Fully recognize and affirm the reaching of goals and meeting of commitments. All your support tactics help students learn to manage their own behavior—a key to their success now and to later success in school, career, and life in general.

In providing such support, you make a critical difference in the young adolescent's life, as explained in *This We Believe: Keys to Educating Young Adolescents* (NMSA, 2010).

> The "hidden curriculum"—what students learn indirectly but surely from the people with whom they interact, the structures in which they work, and the issues that inevitably occur in a human enterprise—has a powerful influence on students' education. In fact, this aspect of learning is sometimes so profound and long lasting that it overrides learning that is more traditional. Lives are often shaped more by small individual actions, probing questions, subtle reminders, earned commendations, and personalized challenges, than by direct instruction. (p. 29)

When the student has lived up to the agreement, thank him or her for the great effort. Make sure to give the rewards that were promised to the student. Make sure to continue to encourage and support the improved behavior that resulted from the intervention. These acts are critical parts of your follow up! Also, invite the student back to a team meeting to talk about his or her accomplishment and the rewards (the concrete rewards earned and other rewards or outcomes of doing a better job with behavior or academics, as well). For the whole class—don't forget to keep class protocols fresh in their minds by reviewing them periodically through puzzles or games.

Follow up with parents. Find out what they are observing and experiencing related to the issue. Let them know what's happening at school. Be sure to compliment their child's growth and progress and their role in helping with the situation.

As a team or other teacher group, take some time to reflect on your intervention plan and process. Adjust and adapt this as needed. Get feedback as to how things worked—from each other, from the students, from parents, and from administrators.

For Reflection and Action

1. Are teachers and teams in your school empowered to handle discipline problems? If not, what are barriers to this and how can they be overcome? If so, what issues still need to be resolved?

2. Do your intervention processes empower students to be accountable for their actions? What improvements would encourage students to take responsibility?

3. Have you tried bringing a student into a meeting where plans regarding his or her behavior or academic issues are discussed? If so, list the beneficial outcomes that resulted. Also list things you learned in the process.

4. If your answer to #3 is no, make a plan with your team to try this process. Make notes about what worked and what didn't.

5. Are your documentation procedures effective and used consistently? If not, what needs to happen to improve this part of the intervention process?

Source: *Managing the Madness: A Practical Guide to Understanding Young Adolescents and Classroom Management*
© Association for Middle Level Education   www.amle.org

CHAPTER 8

The Power of Their Love

Mr. Berckemeyer, I will not sit down, and you can't make me!

The student is right. You can't make a young adolescent student sit down. There are few things you can *make* a student of this age do. (Are there any? Probably not without legal ramifications!) Ultimately, the student has to make his or her own decision about complying with a request from the teacher, doing the school work, behaving with civility, or following class protocols.

Any teacher of young adolescents runs into negative power plays—everything from outright defiance or blatant intimidation to more subtle tactics of procrastination, work avoidance, ignoring, or mumbling criticisms under the breath. Some students focus their power against others they perceive to be weaker. They'll mock the student with the ugly coat or wrong type of clothes or shoes. And heaven forbid another student shows emotion by having a bit of a breakdown in front of others! This desire to pounce on, embarrass, or harass others is all about power. If a student courageously helps another student who appears powerless, the helping student often becomes a target as well, evoking such comments as "How can you help her?" or "Why are you being nice to that freak?" or "Is he your new best friend?"

I'm sure you've said something like this to yourself (probably more than once): "My young adolescent students can be the cruelest people on the face of the earth." And you're right. They can kick a friend's backpack all the way down the hall while calling her an inappropriate name. Feeling guilty, they drop a dollar in the bucket for a world disaster relief effort, and suddenly the guilt seems to be gone!

We're floored by some of these mean, insulting actions. But the next minute, these same kids can amaze us with their capacities for empathy and helpfulness toward others. Young adolescents can be the kindest, most compassionate and giving people on the planet. There are countless stories of heroism by young teens: A 13-year-old, after Hurricane Katrina, became a major figure (and the only child) building a group called the MowRons that worked to mow grass, clean up, and reclaim the local parks of New Orleans (Ellas, 2007). An Illinois teen saved a boy from drowning in the ocean in Hawaii, then swam back out to rescue the boy's father ("Deerfield Teen Saves Drowning Man," 2016). A 15-year-old performed CPR to save a man's life at a Walmart (Robinson, 2016). And these are just a few of many such acts.

Young adolescent students have raised hundreds of thousands of dollars for school playground equipment, local libraries, needy families, and world disaster relief. They've collected canned goods to feed the hungry and volunteered to run clothing drives for the homeless. They've walked, run, biked, swum, bowled, danced, rapped, and sung to raise money for local charities. They've painted murals over graffiti in urban areas and planted gardens to provide fresh produce for families and to beautify inner cities. When exposed to news of a major catastrophe or injustice in the world, they feel pain and sorrow for the less fortunate. In many cases, young adolescents are even keenly aware of the very misuses of power they themselves exhibit! They post videos and other messages on social media denouncing bullying, various kinds of shaming, and school violence—including gun violence, beatings, and teacher bashing. Given opportunities, adolescents make positive changes in their schools, communities, and the world.

Keeping the Balance

All students, particularly at the young adolescent ages, need to gain, feel, and express personal power. This is a natural part of growing up and becoming independent. In this process, many of them will challenge the power of others—especially adults. All teachers will get some pushback from students. There are also some young adolescents who feel too little personal power. The overwhelming changes, new demands, and greater responsibilities leave them feeling anxious and diminished. Instead of challenging others, they withdraw. They have a hard time asserting themselves.

Our job as teachers is to help students develop their own power, take responsibility for it, and learn to manage it in healthy ways for their lives now and in the future. We must commend them for their acts to help people they don't know (campaigning to save the world). At the same time we must help them understand that this is easier than helping others right in front of them or using their power in kind ways in their everyday lives.

We want students to be able to stand up and speak up for themselves and to grow in independence. At the same time, we know it is not good for anybody when the student just rolls over others, asserting power that hurts others. We can't tiptoe around the surly student, ignoring or diminishing the aggressive behavior to avoid confrontation with his or her anger. If teachers do this, we are tellling students that aggression and hostility are powerful, legitimate tools to get whatever they want. Nor can we stand by and let the silent ones continue to feel weak and insignificant. This deepens their powerlessness and leaves them vulnerable to self-doubt and bullying.

We want *all* students to learn ways to challenge the power of others in positive, constructive ways. I hope this chapter will, first of all, inspire you to appreciate (even marvel at) and respect the power of young adolescents. In addition, I'll suggest strategies for empowering students, for nurturing positive uses of their tremendous power, and for responding to their negative uses of power.

Of course, teachers need power too. In too many classrooms, teacher power and student power clash. This does not have to be the case! Teachers and students can share power in ways appropriate for them both. Teachers can find the balance between wielding too much power and too little power. As a teacher, all your efforts to help students develop personal power will not diminish your power—but will deepen it.

Nourishing Positive Use of Power

There's a lot of talk about empowering students. In the most literal sense, *empower* means *to give power or authority to*. I don't want to limit the understanding to this definition. Yes, there are times when you give "authority" (actions that might typically be seen as the teacher's authority) to a student—inviting him or her to teach a lesson or run some function of the classroom. But in most cases, *empowering* students involves a subtler and more important meaning of the word, which is: *to enable someone to be more strong and confident, particularly in controlling her or his own life and actions.* So think of your efforts to *empower* students as nurturing and channeling the power they already (naturally) have.

In his book, *The Classroom of Choice*, Jonathan Erwin (2004) describes three kinds of power: *power over* (the urge to control others perhaps for personal satisfaction or because one believes it's good for the other person); *power within* (power that a person feels or gains from competence or accomplishments); and *power with* (power achieved in cooperation with others). He encourages teachers to provide daily opportunities for students to gain *power within* and *power with*. And I loved when he pointed out that the teacher who lets go of some of the *power over* actually gains power! Here's why: When the teacher backs off from *power over* and practices (and models) *power within* and *power with*, students learn to meet their needs for power through choosing *power within* and *power with* rather than *power over* (pp. 99-117). Everyone wins!

Success at empowering students is rooted in the attitudes, values, norms, and processes of the classroom and school. What follows are some key ways you can nourish students' *power within* and *power with*. You'll probably recognize these themes and suggestions as related to key messages from all the previous chapters in this book.

1. *Honor students' power*. Admire it. Don't fight it or try to diminish it. Relish in the possibilities of what students can do. Let them know you believe they have power and can use it to do wonderful things.

2. *Model fair, respectful, mature uses of power*. Remember this: Every minute of class, students observe how the teacher operates the classroom, relates to each student, and responds to challenges and frustrations. Students notice when a teacher fumes, yells, threatens, or loses it all together! They notice whether the teacher is able to share power with them or whether the teacher needs constant power over them. Yes, there are times as a teacher when you will need to use *power over*. But students should see many examples of the other forms of power.

3. *Establish the tone of the class early*. From the beginning, make it clear that the mindset of this class is to inspire each other to use our personal power in ways that are uplifting or positive for ourselves and for each other.

4. *Build students' sense of belonging*. Consistently find ways to give the message that everyone in the class is a needed and valued member of the group. Reinforce actions that show that in this class, we stick up for each other. Hold discussions about this topic. Ask students what happens in the class that lets them know they belong (or makes them doubt it). Let them suggest ways to let everyone know he or she belongs. Recognize the important elements that different students contribute to the class. Have students look for and point out the value of their peers to the group. Do your best to get students in the habit of looking for ways to nurture each other. For example, students can celebrate

each others' birthdays by decorating their desks, cubbies, or lockers (with decorations that include compliments and encouraging messages).

5. *Attend to relationship building and classroom safety.* According to the William Glasser's Choice Theory (1999), the first of the five basic needs that drive humans is the need to survive (pp.25-43). Positive power is drained away when any person feels anxious, insecure, or threatened. To be empowered positively, students need to be able to count on the fact that the teacher knows and likes them, and consistently promotes, expects, and defends caring, fair, and kind relationships.

6. *Reinforce positive demonstrations of power.* Notice and practice concrete actions that deepen the message that it's important to help everyone feel powerful. Encourage students to pick up others' papers when they fall to the floor or help each other in many small and big ways. Be direct: if you know of a student who gets picked on, ask another student to take him a pencil that you have provided. Simple gestures can make a world of difference in some students' lives. Celebrate student's accomplishments and efforts at healthy power use. Let students nominate a Student of the Week. Each week, change the criteria so that they must look for a wide variety of attributes in their peers. Let students brainstorm kinds of actions or attributes for a list of criteria.

> Of course, letting some of the power in the classroom go to the students may cause angst for the teacher! Young adolescents will try to exert their power in any way they can. The question becomes, 'Do you want to facilitate and direct their use of power or let them control the process?'

7. *Share ownership of the class.* Make sure every student sees this as "our class" and not "Mrs. or Ms. or Mr. So-and- So's class." Ask yourself, "Do I really believe the class is theirs as much as mine?" and "What have I done to convince them of that?" (Note: Strategies that promote students' voices, choices, competence, and leadership go a long way toward increasing their feeling of ownership.)

8. *Let students know that their voices matter.* Give students multiple and regular ways to express their ideas, opinions, accomplishments, and experiences; share what they learn; take part in decision making; and contribute to planning learning activities and classroom procedures. Hold class meetings where students discuss and solve problems about classroom issues. Have a regular place or procedure for students to make suggestions. Give surveys that ask for students' input on classroom matters. See to it that all students have a part in making decisions—real-life decisions that matter. It is empowering for students (and all human beings!) when someone listens to them. So listen to students and help them listen to each other.

9. *Offer choices.* Every day, plan situations in which students have choices—in planning lessons or learning strategies, in establishing classroom procedures, in setting goals, in determining what they learn, in deciding how they learn, and in choosing how they show what they learn. Offer choices in things they read, projects they do, or rewards they work for. Let them choose the order for doing work tasks. Give choices in assignments and test questions. Do you want to know if you're truly giving students choice? Ask them! Here's the answer you want to hear: "Yes, we have choices all the time."

10. *Make room for your students' autonomy.* Nurture their autonomy (their ability to think, make decisions, feel, and act on their own). A huge part of the young adolescent's growing up is learning to handle the complexities of their expanding independence. Help your students explore, develop, practice, and test skills of coping with the new challenges of autonomy. The more success a growing adolescent has at using autonomy in healthy ways, the deeper will be his or her positive uses of power.

11. *Work to help each student build competence.* Consciously or unconsciously, students constantly evaluate whether they can succeed at learning tasks. This is their assessment of their personal competence. When the student's answer to herself of himself is, "Yes, I can do this!" the student gains power. This in turn translates into higher levels of engagement in learning activities, which contributes to even more competence. Foster the sense of competence for each student. Assign tasks that give a slight challenge so the student needs to stretch, but give feedback, scaffolding, and support to help the student succeed. Succeeding at learning is absolutely one of the most effective ways to develop positive power within.

12. *Build leadership.* Give every student chances to lead. Brainstorm different kinds of leadership roles and rotate students in these roles. Give students opportunities to teach something to other students, to a group, or to the whole class. Let them take leadership roles in planning a curriculum lesson, leading a class meeting, or advising the team. Empower students with tasks that make them leaders of groups, events, regular duties, or organizational tasks.

13. *Affirm students to their parents.* What a way to help a student feel powerful! Take the time to send home a note, email, or text—or to make a brief phone call—to brag about a student's accomplishments or awesome, positive uses of power. Do this often for every student.

14. *Address misuses of power.* Although it is difficult, address students' power plays, mean comments, and inappropriate gestures and facial expressions. When they occur, discuss them with the student right away. Response to negative power plays and power struggles is discussed later in this chapter. But I put it here in the "positive" section, because part of nurturing positive uses of power is heightening awareness to the harmful uses of power.

15. *Empower students in team meetings.* An intervention or misbehavior is not the only reason to bring a student into a meeting of the team's teachers. A "team talk" is a great way to motivate students and increase their power. Here are a few (of many) ways to involve students in team meetings:

- Following a lesson, unit, or project, invite a few students to a team meeting to discuss the event. (This is much like a focus group.) Ask for their input on the subject matter, the assignments, the final project, or the assessment. If they know you are open to their honest feedback, most adolescents will share their opinions and discuss their likes and dislikes concerning the lesson.

- Ask students to help create a unit of study. They can participate in team meetings, cooperating with the teachers to devise lessons and activities.

- Have students practice their social and presentation skills by bringing to the team their ideas for celebrations and rewards.

- Students can practice problem solving and collaboration by sharing ideas about how to spruce up the hallways, eliminate tardiness, clean up perpetual messes in the lunchroom or hallways, or find solutions to other school needs or issues.

- At the end of the year, invite some students who have performed well all year to a team meeting. Ask them what they liked about the year. This will be powerful for the students and a boost for you. (It might even stop your eyelid twitch for a few days.) Try the same process with students who might have struggled in some ways. Ask the same question. You might be surprised by what you learn. Asking for their feedback will really empower these kids!

16. *Address adolescent power across the school.* Create an advisory program or curriculum concentrated on helping others. Create building-wide programs wherein all members of the school community learn about, discuss, and collaborate to support each other in the quest to replace negative with positive use of power.

All of the above tactics help to build the healthy, productive, and appropriate uses of young adolescent power. And here's the bonus: At the same time, they all diminish negative uses of power. When students get their needs for power met through legitimate means, there is much less of a chance that power will push its way out in harmful ways. Every chapter in this book leads to this. All those strategies and attitudes for proactive classroom management really do make a difference in how young adolescents feel, gain, and demonstrate their power.

Activity to Empower Students

Here's a sample power-sharing activity. (See Figure 8.1, "Sample Review Activity". Lessons like this increase motivation and class participation and help students channel their power into self-reliance and decision-making. This is a language arts example, but the idea can be adapted to any subject area.

Teacher information:
1. Tell your students that each of them has the goal of accumulating 60 points during the allotted time (a class period, perhaps). Each individual selects tasks, choosing any combination of activities as long as they add up to 60 points. (Points, of course, are contingent upon full and satisfactory completion of the tasks.)

2. The list of possible tasks is endless. Assign the point values according to the time, creativity, thought, complexity of research, and detail that the task will require. Students review and deepen content while working on a combination of tasks that suits their natural interests, abilities, and skills. Give gentle guidance to help students who need it. Don't hesitate to nudge students to challenge themselves.

Figure 8-1 *Sample Review Activity*

Review Activity

Directions: Read the short story "Why Ants Burn So Quickly" (a fictitious story, by the way). Then choose and complete activities from the list below to equal 60 points.

- Answer the five questions at the end of the short story. Do this in writing or on an audio recording. Point value: 25

- Review the story's vocabulary list on page 49 of your text. Define each word and use it in a sentence that relates to school. At least five of the sentences must be questions. You can include more than one vocabulary word in a sentence. Point value: 20

- Create a menu using the information from the story "Why Ants Burn So Quickly". Be creative with your menu items. Point value: 20

- Write a short story about the life of an ant. Include at least two characters and the plot elements of introduction, conflict or problem, turning point, and resolution. Point value: 40

- Using the Internet, research information on ants. Compile a list of ten key or surprising facts about ants. Point value: 5 for each reference; limit 20 points

- Create a detailed, well-labeled diagram of an ant's body and features. Within the diagram, briefly identify the function of each feature. Point value: 10

- Write a well-developed fiction or nonfiction paragraph on how ants help humans. Point value: 10

- List ten reasons why people hate ants. Point value: 5

Source: *Managing the Madness: A Practical Guide to Understanding Young Adolescents and Classroom Management*
© Association for Middle Level Education   www.amle.org

Handling Negative Uses of Power

You've seen all kinds of misuses of power by young adolescents (if you're a parent, you've seen it double!)— the nastiness to peers, sullen uncooperativeness, sarcasm, defiance, and putdowns.

Some of the unsuitable uses of power are subtle or passive. I'm sure you recognize the following tactics. If you confront a student on one of these, you'll probably get the response, "What? I'm not doing anything!"

- Procrastinating (taking as much time as possible to complete a two-minute task or to start or finish any activity)

- Wandering around and looking for something to do or someone to bother

- Acting like she or he did not hear the question

- Making the famous "I don't get it" statement

- Rolling the eyes

- Constantly looking disgusted—the rolled-up nose and wrinkly forehead (which will result in horrible lines when they are older)

- Using confrontational or intimidating looks

- Demonstrating an "I don't care" attitude verbally or nonverbally

- Resorting to the all-too-familiar, "Whatever!"

- Refusing to work

- Repeating annoying behaviors like burping or desk banging

- Saying "This is dumb!" (or writing it on the assignment)

- Saying "You're not fair!"

- Asking "What are we supposed to do?" after you've just explained what to do

Some of the negative power use is more outwardly belligerent or aggressive:

- Fighting

- Pushing someone or something

- Tripping someone

- Intimidating someone with under-the-breath mutterings, threatening notes (or tweets or texts), or audible comments

- Poking or hitting someone with a pencil, ruler, or any available object

- Using inappropriate language

- Swinging of the arms toward others

- Making derogatory remarks

- Using confrontational gestures

- Flauntingly breaking clear rules or expectations

What's a teacher to do? Many of the ideas related to behavior management in previous chapters apply to these power plays. I'm sure you have a list of strategies you've used and found effective (or dropped because they didn't work). Of course, no one response is appropriate for every incident or every student. Here are some general principles, strategies, and suggestions:

Ignore it. There are times when the best response is no response. See the section "The Art of Ignoring" below.

Plan ahead. Have a repertoire of strategies at hand for interrupting the behavior or redirecting and refocusing the student to something else. For example: Give nonverbal clues. Move close to the student. Change the student's location. Change the task. Give the student or the class a break.

Get a full picture of the behavior. If the behavior is pervasive, find out why the student is seeking to gain power in this way. What purpose is this serving for the student? Is it organic hyperactivity? Is it restlessness because there hasn't been a brain or body break recently? Has something traumatic or hurtful happened recently for the student? Is the student in desperate need of attention? Is the task too difficult or confusing for the student? Is this happening in other classes? If you get to the root of the behavior, you'll get a clearer sense of how to respond.

Hold to your established classroom protocols. If the students have been well informed that a behavior is not okay for your classroom, follow through on the stated rules and consequences. As soon as you start slipping on consistency with carrying out consequences, the protocols lose meaning. DO review the rules often. DO conduct behavior rehearsals.

Keep a check on your own use of power. There are times when your power is challenged. These are exactly the situations in which you teach students the most about power by the way you respond. Keep your sense of self and your sense of humor. Don't slam things down on your desk, stomp your foot, rant, or pout. Don't take the behavior personally—even if it is directed at you. Be an adult. Keep your exasperation under wraps (even if she's banged the table 1,000 times). Respond calmly and evenly.

Don't further diminish the student's power. Choose responses that don't put down, embarrass, or denigrate the student. Powerlessness creates anxiety, and often, revenge. Any response that embarrasses or demeans the student deepens the problem. Inappropriate uses of power are ready-made chances to help students gain positive power. Respond in ways that help the student make good choices—thus increasing her or his sense of autonomy. You'll read examples of this as you continue with this chapter.

The Art of Ignoring

If you responded to every irksome behavior, you'd never finish a lesson! Ignore minor irritants. Often, after a short period of increase (the student has to get in those last five desk bangs), the action stops. Ignoring generally works best if the behavior is motivated by a need for attention from you or peers. If you've talked ahead of time with your class about the importance of not egging on annoying behavior, other students will likely see that you're ignoring it and will follow your lead. When the behavior doesn't get the desired attention, it will often stop.

Ignore wisely. If the action obviously and repeatedly violates a rule, if it becomes harmful to that student or a peer, or if it impedes learning for the class, you'll need to respond.

Sometimes ignoring makes the student feel resentful or unimportant. The behavior might escalate. Watch out for this. Within a short time, follow your initial lack of verbal response with some validation to the student. You might move near him, pat her on the shoulder, or make a brief encouraging comment about the work the student is doing.

That Pesky Procrastination

How to deal with student procrastination is the million-dollar question because the behavior is usually passive and not as "in your face" as many other power plays. Young adolescents have mastered the art of drawing out a ten-minute lesson into a week's worth of work. Here are some typical ways they avoid working and some strategies you might want to try:

- The "stealth method" is the most common tactic used by young adolescents. A student scans the room while pretending to work. Instead of working, she or he is actually focusing in on the next target—someone easy to pick on. When the selected target walks by, the student pokes or kicks the target or makes a mean comment hoping to coax an eruption from the other person. The target can be anyone who happens to be in the vicinity.

- Pretending to write, draw, or organize themselves are other common strategies. This includes paper shuffling, losing materials, and pawing through backpacks and desks—accompanied by lots of moans, sighs, groans, and talking to self.

- Other familiar procrastination methods include staring at the pencil to see if it has grown in the last several minutes, the "Oops, I dropped my piece of paper again" comments, sharpening of pencils, using a hall pass to roam the halls, asking repeated questions to get the teacher's attention, and introducing a topic that gets the teacher off the subject.

Try these tactics for managing and diminishing procrastination:

- The teacher plays a critical role in the pacing and motivation of students. If you want kids to work, you have to work the room. Pretend it is the cocktail party you never get invited to because you are too busy sleeping or grading papers on the weekends. Mingle! Walk around and greet everyone. Participate in small talk with your students. Pretend you own the room—after all, you are a co-owner anyway! This allows you to make sure work is being done.

- If students are not working productively, tell them you are not letting them leave until they finish the first set of questions. Then make sure you hold them accountable. (See the upcoming section "Accountability—It's Non-negotiable.")

- At the beginning of class, give students only half of the assignment, quiz, or other task; later give them the other half. This counters the students' tendencies to look at the time in a class period and the number of questions and feel, "I will never finish this in time." For some students that list of 20 questions is overwhelming, and they shut down before they even start. Breaking the assignment into smaller sections helps them gain skills in pacing themselves, problem solving, and test taking—all of which build confidence and self-esteem while challenging their defeatist attitudes.

- Occasionally, tell students that the first half of the assignment is for a grade and the last half is for bonus points. It is amazing how many want that extra credit.

- Turn the assignment into a scavenger hunt. When they finish one part of the task, they go around the room to hunt for the next question or part of the task. In most cases, adding the goal of moving and finding something cuts procrastination to zero.

- Have you ever noticed that when you are energized and ready to go, your students' attitudes and motivation will follow? (It's like being jacked up on Red Bull and Mountain Dew.) Don't hesitate to tell your students there is so much to do today that they'll have to keep moving quickly. Remember, many of them are comfortable multitasking with electronics and juggling several pieces of information at once. Once you get their attention, you can then break things down into smaller pieces.

- Start class by saying, "We have a million things to do today." Write on the board a list of 10 items that students need to complete by the end of the day, and don't worry about overwhelming them. Here is the important part: of the list of 10 items, only 5 are real. Your students will never know that some of the assignments are fake. They have no idea that "Reflection Sheet A97.2" does not exist. Then, as the students behave and start to work, erase some of the fake assignments. Tell them it is a reward for working responsibly.

- Keep trays in the back of the room (near the door) with handouts, assignments, or graded work. Students can pick these up when they enter the room. This prevents them from taking forever to distribute papers.

Let's stop basing student achievement on a bell that rings every 55 minutes. Students with the ability to complete assigned work in the class period should be expected to do so. Teach students that NOT completing work (or completing it sloppily) isn't an option.

Accountability: It's Non-negotiable

In middle schools and high schools, students expect to be allowed to leave the classroom when the bell rings. Unless the class is right before essentials classes or lunch (when a teacher could keep students past the bell to complete assignments), students usually transition to the next class whether or not they have completed their work. However, holding your students accountable is critical to their development of responsibility, future success, and positive use of power.

I remember a procrastinating (and, yes, lazy) student who repeatedly did not complete his work. In fact, he would not even put a heading on the paper, although he was fully capable of finishing the assignment. My teammates and I decided that he would remain in language arts class to finish his work—even if the bell had rung. The student ended up staying in that class all day, and much to my shock and dismay, he still had done nothing. But here is the amazing part: I met him when he got off the bus the following morning, and he came in and finished the assignment. It took him five minutes.

Pleased with this success, I optimistically tried the approach with another student. The outcome was the same: she finished her work. Interestingly, after sitting in the class for three periods, she began to answer the questions before any of the other students had a chance to respond. After hearing the same lesson three times that day, the message sank in. She functioned like the brightest kid in the class. Of course, students eventually figured out the system and used it to avoid attending classes they didn't like and to disrupt the classes taking place where they were held back.

Before using this tactic, make sure you cover all the bases. Discuss the tough, practical issues regarding this process with your teammates and determine on a case-by-case basis which students would be helped most by this approach. Start small, and then build on your success. If the approach does not work, or if it becomes misused by the student, try something different for a while. You can always come back to this tactic later in the year with another student.

Before holding a student in a class to finish work, consider such questions as these with your teammates:

1. Why is the student not doing the work? Is it because the level is too high or is the student just lazy? Is there an emotional reason such as trouble at home or with another student? Or is there another reason for acting out? (The top priority is to address any underlying issues. For example, if you're asking a

student to do something in a class period that is not possible for her to do in that time, then you'll need to adjust the assignment.)

2. How will the student make up missed work from the other core classes? Or should that missing work be made up at all?

3. What will be the impact on essentials or exploratory classes? When you ask the music, art, PE, or exploratory teacher about this, do not do it in an email. Go have a face-to-face talk with that teacher and explain what you are trying to accomplish.

4. For which students will this process work? For which will it not work?

5. How do we evaluate the process to see if it is working?

6. Do we do this with a select group of students or with any student in the group?

7. How do we involve and inform parents and administrators?

Power Struggles

The teacher makes a request. The student refuses, ignores, or defies. The teacher gets louder and more aggressive; the face gets red. The student gets more combative; he has to save face. The scene escalates. A simple request has become an emotionally charged standoff.

My first bit of advice about power struggles is this: don't get into them. Everybody loses in a power struggle (including the students observing it and all those students who hear about it second-hand in a matter of minutes through digital messages).

My second bit of advice is this: the way you react to the student's refusal, ignoring, or defiance sets an example for all the students in the room of what to do when someone defies them (passively or aggressively) and of how to handle their feelings in such situations.

So here are some do's and don'ts for avoiding and responding to power confrontations:

- The best way to prevent defiance and power grabs is to give students plenty of ways and chances to exercise personal power constructively.

- Don't react to every little issue or comment. Avoid getting any struggle started by not letting a student draw you in. As much as you can, rely on the relationship you have with the student and what you know about the student to keep from pushing his or her buttons and triggering hostility.

- Disengage from a brewing power struggle. Try to stop the behavior and handle it later with a talk. Interrupt an escalating situation by redirecting the student to something else, sending the student on an errand, or taking a class brain break.

- The student's need to assert herself in a power play often flows from a sense of inadequacy. Try to remove the reinforcement that students get from negative power plays. Your disengagement tactics (as above) can also disengage the peer reinforcement the student is getting in the situation.

- Resist the urge to stop the confrontation by sending the student to the office. Try to keep her or him in class. The student misses out on valuable learning while sitting in the principal's office.

- Before such confrontations arise, let your students know that you will respond. Tell them something like this: "It's my responsibility to let you know when you are disrespectful, harmful, or diminishing of yourself or others. I take that responsibility seriously and I will not overlook such actions."

- Remain calm—no voice-raising, no angry gestures. Take a deep breath. State the expectation ONCE in a neutral, even voice. Give the student a chance to use his or her own self-control to get back to work or comply with the request.

- Forget about having the last word. Kids will have it anyway. Even if the student complies, he'll probably have the last word with a "whatever" muttered under the breath or a nasty look behind your back.

You can't avoid power plays or quickly interrupt or divert the student's defiance all the time. And students won't always ditch the power play with your one calm reminder. When the defiance continues past your statement of the expectation, you'll need to address the student in private. If the situation allows everyone to carry on with the class so that you can talk to the student later, catch the student after class to set a time for that. If not, try to find a way to speak quietly with the student in or near the classroom. This might be with the student in the hall and you standing in the doorway. As a last resort, send the student away from the classroom (to the office, or "on loan" to a teacher friend to do a job in that classroom) and talk to the student later.

It's good to give the student some time and space to sit by himself or herself before you talk. This lets the student cool down (and you, too). Do this if you have a place for the student and a situation where the student isn't disruptive.

When you talk to the student, whether it is in the corner of the room, in the hall, or in a conference after school:

- Stay cool and calm.

- Stay connected to the student. Remember what you know about this student.

- Sit down beside the student on an even level.

- Give the student physical space. Don't get in her or his face.

- Slow down. Talk slowly.

- Be kind, caring, and respectful.

- Don't debate or argue.

- Don't manipulate the student emotionally with guilt or disappointment.

- Don't try to reason.

- Don't use "you" statements.

- Don't say "don't" or "you always.... ."

- Don't lecture.

- Don't use sarcasm.

- Don't negotiate.

- Don't ask why the student behaved as she or he did. Ask this instead: "Can you help me understand what happened?"

- Let the student talk. Listen. You may learn something very important about what's behind the behavior. Try to understand the student and the actions.

- Repeat the expectation and the consequence.

- State the choices: "You can do ____ or ____."

- Avoid ultimatums.

- Always give the student a way to rectify the situation.

- Give the student a way to save face.

- Use humor to defuse the tension.

- Let the student have the last word.

- Allow the student to recover pride and to have hope that he or she can do better. Once the issue is addressed, drop it. Don't carry this over to the next class or day. Make it clear to the student (and all students) that tomorrow is a new day.

Parent Power

Young adolescents crave power and seek it both at home and at school. Anyone who has raised a young adolescent knows that the mood of the child can dictate the mood of an entire house. As a teacher, you can also witness how power can affect a family. How many times have you heard a parent say, "I don't know what to do with her"? You are thinking, "She is 12; how can you have given your power to a 12-year-old?" Young adolescent power, used poorly, can frustrate parents, teachers, and the student as well.

Without a doubt, parents are regularly challenged in their daily interactions with their developing young adolescent children. Teachers and parents (or guardians) need to support each other as much as possible. Some parents are afraid of teachers and the school; some are suspicious—perhaps they had bad experiences in school, or they may speak little or no English. Parents sometimes feel defensive and withdraw if they do not feel safe relating to the teacher and school. A large body of research shows that students whose parents are involved in their school lives (as opposed to students whose parents are not) achieve greater academic success and are more likely to go on to postsecondary education. This is true regardless of socioeconomic background. Thus, it is critical that we identify any barriers to parent involvement and try to break these down.

Remember that, for each child in your room, there is someone for whom that child is their world—someone who values that child as deeply as his or her own life. That is powerful. When combined, the power of parents and the power of teachers—focused on making school the best possible experience for that student—is awesome. Keep parent power in your mind as you work to help students gain and use power effectively and humanely.

Most parents want to do a good job of parenting. In most cases, they'll be grateful for any suggestions teachers can offer them. I know that sometimes getting even a few parents to show up at a meeting can be challenging. But there are many other ways to share ideas with parents—even with those who aren't actively seeking your help. Here are two samples of some information and tips you might share with students' parents or guardians. Figure 8-1 has general suggestions for all parents of adolescents. Figure 8-2 is adapted from tips that former middle school teacher and administrator Judith Baenen created for parents of middle level students. The suggestions are certainly also applicable and adaptable to parents of adolescents well past middle school.

You can send such tips as these home by mail, share them on your class website, include them in a regular newsletter, or email them to parents. If you give them to students to take home, count on maybe five percent of the sheets actually getting into parents' hands!

Figure 8-1

How to Raise an Adolescent without Going Crazy

- Be consistent. 10:00 pm means 10:00 pm—no exceptions. The more consistent you are, the easier it is for the young adolescent to live up to your expectations.

- Teach kids to say, "I feel…, I need…, I want…"

- Check up on them. Don't hesitate to call to make sure they went where they said they were going.

- Don't take their behavior or challenges personally. The mood of your son or daughter should not control the mood of the entire house. Wait a few minutes and the child's mood will change.

- Keep the school backpack cleaned out. A weekly cleaning will turn up missing assignments, notices of upcoming important school events, and dirty plastic containers with moldy science projects in them.

- Talk with other parents and form your own support system. Find out what methods they are using effectively. Get together and discuss strategies or read and discuss good articles or books.

- Use the school schedule as the basis for making a personal planner for your child. Add important extracurricular activities and family commitments.

- Enjoy their humor. The young adolescent years can be a fun time for kids as their senses of humor develop. Don't be afraid to laugh with them.

- Keep your eye on their technology use. It is very important to help your child learn the appropriate uses and dangers of their digital world. Don't be afraid to set limits on screen time. Don't be afraid to use the blocking devices to keep your child off dangerous sites. Don't be afraid to monitor their social network use and other Internet use. You probably pay the bill for the cell phone or Internet access. Cutting off access is a powerful tool. Use it to keep your child safe.

- Keep in touch with the school—remember, there are always two sides to a story. Talk to the teacher and get his or her input before rushing to judgment about incidents at school.

- And, finally, remember—you are the parent.

Source: *Managing the Madness: A Practical Guide to Understanding Young Adolescents and Classroom Management*
© Association for Middle Level Education   www.amle.org

Figure 8-2

Tips for Living Successfully with Your Middle Level Student

Think ahead. One of the best tips for parents is "be prepared." As your son or daughter enters the middle school years, get ready for at least occasional conflicts. Think through what is truly important to you. Is the hairstyle as important as the homework? Isn't curfew more of a concern than crabbiness? Obviously, dawdling is a lot easier to accept than drugs. As these give-and-take situations start, know ahead of time which areas you are willing to negotiate and which areas are absolute.

Break down big chores into small parts. Sometimes young people feel overwhelmed by tasks, especially those they've let go for a long time. A disastrous bedroom, 23 overdue math assignments, a long-term project that's "suddenly" due in a few days (or hours!)—all of these can lead a young adolescent to give up rather than get started.

Help your child by setting up smaller goals. These goals are attainable: Clean off your bed. Get five assignments done tonight. Gather the materials for the project. Young adolescents have trouble structuring tasks so that they are more approachable. Parents can help them in this.

Encourage your middle schooler to keep a daily to-do list (weekly is too much). You may need to assign a specific time to each task. When the task is completed, the student draws a line through it.

Remind your middle schooler about appointments and due dates. Think ahead about materials required for a project (unless you look forward to late-evening visits to the store). This will not last forever. When this same child was learning to walk, we held her hands and made the path smooth. Now she is learning to take on a tremendous assortment of life tasks and changes. Handholding (but not the firm, physical grip previously necessary) is needed for about a year or so as your middle schooler gets started on the road to being more responsible and mature.

Be willing to listen—but don't poke or pry. Kids this age value independence and often seem secretive. Keeping to themselves is part of the separateness they are trying to create. Let them know you'd love to help them, but don't push them into a defensive position. (Of course, you'll have to pry when their safety is at risk.)

If your child is in the midst of a longtime friendship that is falling apart, the best thing you can do is stand by and be a good listener. It is devastating for us to see our children hurting, but taking sides or intervening is not appropriate. Nor will it help. Young adolescents do survive these hurts, especially if they know we are there to listen to their pain.

Figure 8-2 *Tips for Living Successfully with Your Middle Level Student, continued*

Help them gain perspective. Young adolescents need to learn that being "best friends" isn't always smooth sailing. People have differences of opinion and even get angry with one another, but they still care for each other. When kids are involved in those "I-hate-her-she-is-so-stuck-up" and "How-could-she-do-this-to-me?" conversations, parents must help them see that one problem need not ruin a relationship, but stubbornness might. Middle schoolers have a lot of spats and falling outs, but, often, the friends are back together in a short time.

Accept them for who they are. Listen. Don't needlessly criticize. Back them up when they're right. Pick them up when they're down.

When reprimanding, deal only with the precise problem. Don't bring in other issues. "The trash is still here, and it needs to go out now" is better than, "You are so lazy! I told you to take the trash out two hours ago, and it's still here! You'd live in a pigsty, wouldn't you? Well, you aren't the only one in this house, you know..."

If the issue is minor, keep things light. The shoes on the floor, the wet towel on the bed, the carton left open—these are maddening, perhaps, but not earth-shattering. Call attention to them in a humorous way so that your young adolescent knows you want action but you aren't being punitive. "Either the cat's smarter than I thought, or you left the milk carton open on the counter. One of you please put it back before it spoils."

Don't use power unless it's urgent. Parents have the ultimate power, and kids know it. We don't have to "prove" it to them at every turn. Save your strength for those really important issues you've decided are non-negotiable. Eventually, kids are going to possess power of their own, and we want them to be able to use it wisely.

Source: *Managing the Madness: A Practical Guide to Understanding Young Adolescents and Classroom Management*
© Association for Middle Level Education   www.amle.org

For Reflection and Action

1. Describe two strategies you have used successfully to help students develop healthy uses of power. What other strategies or approaches from this chapter will you try?

2. For one week, keep track of the power struggles that students present. Make notes about how you handle these. Reflect on what you did that worked and what you'll do differently next week.

3. Reflect on how you feel about the idea of sharing ownership of the class or turning over some of your power to students. What scares you about this? What excites you about this?

4. For two weeks, notice the times a student exerts negative power and you fail to intervene. What are the barriers to intervening? With a colleague, brainstorm how to overcome those barriers.

5. How well does your school community collaborate and act to address the topics of empowering students positively and responding to student power plays? Does your faculty consistently model (to students and to each other) mature, humane uses of power?

Source: *Managing the Madness: A Practical Guide to Understanding Young Adolescents and Classroom Management*
© Association for Middle Level Education   www.amle.org

CHAPTER 9

Living the Dream

Mr. Berckemeyer, for someone as old as you, you're kinda cool.

When we began our teaching careers with that wide-eyed optimism, we all had a few ace-in-the-hole lessons sure to motivate young adolescents. We envisioned students sitting on the edges of their seats, drawn into our subject matter by their burning desire to know everything about gas, combustibles, and other things that blow up, and by our riveting teaching ability. This was our dream—the reason we went into teaching—to make a difference in the lives of each and every one of our students.

Then, reality set in. We wonder why kids don't get excited about the hands-on activity we have spent hours preparing. We get frustrated as "the perfect" lesson bombs. I once created a lesson so cool (I even wore an outrageous costume for dramatic effect), only to hear the familiar grumblings of restless middle school students saying, "We did this last year. And Ms. Cervantes, our sixth grade teacher, wore a better costume."

I did not accept defeat. Nor did I take it personally. (Well, maybe a little!) What I did do was make some adjustments to the lesson and teach it five days later to the same students. This second time, they were a little more eager, and the lesson seemed to go over fairly well. You just never know for sure how it is going to work out. You just have to keep trying.

Yes, reality does set in for the new teacher. For most, it doesn't take long. It seems that the dream about what we could accomplish as teachers doesn't coexist with reality. But I'd like to argue that we teachers of young adolescents *are living the dream.* It's just different from what we envisioned. Actually, the real life of teaching young adolescents is *better than* our original fresh-out-of-college imaginings. (Okay, I admit our dreams may have sometimes included a bit of mutiny, quitting, running away to Tahiti, or drinking.)

But here we are, spending our days with these amazing, changing, constantly stimulating adolescents!! We marvel at their energy, skills, cleverness, and humor. They shock us with their insights, inventiveness, and honesty. They surprise us with their questions, curiosity, and dedication to things of their interest. No day with them is the same as any other day. We get to witness their limitless possibilities and rejoice in their promise. And best of all, we get to *be* integral players in their dreams! Now isn't that *living your dream*?

So, keep on being creative and keep moving forward. Yes, there will be a daily barrage of adolescent angst. Yes, many lessons will be criticized before you even begin. Remember this about young adolescents: in a little while their fear that everyone is watching them will slowly wither away, leaving you to more easily engage them in creative activities. Listen to your students and trust your instincts. Never stop trying. Believe in your students and make a difference—and have some fun along the way.

Other Final Thoughts

Classroom management is all about how teachers and students spend time together in classrooms and how things work to affect the lives and learning of all the occupants. Life in a classroom with young adolescents can be complicated, dynamic, messy, exhilarating, noisy, heartening, heartwarming, or disheartening. Combine new ideas from this book with your own successful strategies and deep care for your students to create a dynamic mixture of practices that meets the needs of your young adolescent students.

In closing, I leave you with a few last tips that re-emphasize previous thoughts in this book (plus a few others). I so fervently believe these are needed for a healthy, productive life with your students that I'll risk some repetition.

- The more you care about young adolescents and enjoy being with them, the easier it is to be an effective educator for them. They make good company, they tell hilarious stories, they are kind and compassionate, they are fun, and they are willing to help make a difference. Every minute you spend building relationships generates more minutes of quality classroom time and years of benefits to the individual student.

- Do your part to protect and nurture every student in the school. Give affirmations wherever you move about the school. Don't overlook inappropriate comments or behavior. Don't pretend not to see a student trip another student in the hall. Don't walk away when you notice a student harming another student or being self-destructive to himself or herself. Respond! When someone is intimidating, rude, or threatening—stop and talk to that student. Advocate for and protect all students. Remember: It takes a village to raise a child; do your part.

- Over and over, talk to your students as a group about courtesy, decency, and respect. (They may seem to tune you out; but never fear, the message is getting through.) This is a part of your responsibility to help foster ethical and caring individuals. Teaching the expectations for good citizenship does not end after the first week of school. Remember to review, restate, explore, and practice these all year. Remember to model such behavior yourself—all year.

- Take care not to sabotage a colleague. Never say, "I don't care what you do in Mr. Yellico's class." Or, when students say, "Ms. Kovach lets us," your normal reaction might be to say, "Do I look like Ms. Kovach?" You may say something to imply other classes are not as important as yours or other teachers are not as competent as you. When you make statements disrespecting other teachers, you model that behavior for students. There are enough people bashing teachers. We need not do it to each other. And there is hardly a better behavior model for students to see than the respect their teachers show for one another.

- Don't talk too much. Most teachers talk too much. Don't just railroad ahead with a lecture when kids aren't listening or put all kinds of stuff up on a screen that students can't even read or that bores them (while the teacher is not noticing.) Stop and listen and notice. Ask for student feedback.

- Give students time to think. Young adolescents need time to ponder questions, ideas, and new concepts. They need time to reflect before they answer or act. They need time to dig into their memories for information and time to process that information. Give young adolescents at least ten seconds for something they've heard, seen, or read to sink in. Give them longer to form responses. Be patient!

- Unless you're sitting to work with a group of students, don't stop moving. All kinds of personal, emotional, social, and educational things are accomplished by your closeness to students and your movement around the room. (Hey, you get more steps on your fitness tracker too!) Your students, not your projector, need your presence.

- It's wonderful to have an attractive, colorful, creative classroom. It's desirable to use projected lessons and activities with interesting visuals. But visual clutter confuses and distracts students. Display no images or information without a specific educational purpose. Don't put too much information on the interactive whiteboard, display boards, screen, or any other visual teaching surface. Make it easy for students to figure out exactly what the problem is to work on, what word or phrase is being discussed, or what concept is being reviewed.

- Treasure your colleagues. You and they are one another's support system. Be as good at cooperation and collaboration as you hope your students can learn to be. Colleagues saved my proverbial life—many times. Trust each other, work together, learn from each other, challenge each other, and comfort each other.

- Keep your hands clean. Fewer germs means fewer sick days, which results in fewer substitute plans. Also, drink tons of water. According to ear, nose, and throat doctors, teaching is the number two profession for vocal chord abuse. (Singing is number one.)

- Control what you can control and let go of what you cannot. As Debbie Silver, Judith Baenen, and I advise in our book *Deliberate Optimism*, nothing stresses teachers like trying to engineer, fix, and change things out of our control. There are so many things you CAN do. Learn to find joy and fulfillment in diving into those and letting go of those you can't change.

- Laugh. Deliberately include some humor in every class and every lesson. Enjoy your students' humor (as best you can!). Laugh with your students. Laugh with your colleagues. Laugh at yourself. Remember all the healthy benefits of humor. Don't start or end your day without it.

Appendix A

Characteristics and Needs of Young Adolescents

Characteristics of Young Adolescents

Intellectually, young adolescents . . .

- Are egocentric.

- Argue to convince others of their ideas.

- Have frequently fluctuating interests.

- Are dominated by personal social concerns. (Academics are secondary.)

- Are developing critical thinking and independent thinking.

- At times, have difficulty acquiring new conceptual skills.

- Are intensely curious.

- Are easily discouraged if not able to achieve.

- Vary widely in expressions of creativity.

- Are moving toward abstract ways of thinking and thus are able to:
    — Project thoughts into the future.
    — Establish goals.
    — Consider ideas contrary to facts.
    — Question attitudes, behaviors, and values.
    — Think about thinking and how they learn (metacognition).

- Prefer active over passive learning activities.

- Are willing to learn when learning is relevant and meaningful to them.

- Trust adults to help them form moral boundaries.

- Prefer cooperative over individual learning activities.

- Enjoy discussing personal experiences and ideas with adults.

- Relate to abstract ideas such as honesty, fairness, and liberty.

- Are capable of a good deal of independent learning.

- Are enmeshed with technology.

- Relate to learning skills that apply to real life problems and situations.

- Can accept personal responsibility for their learning.

Physically, young adolescents . . .

- Are in the midst of major physical changes.

- Experience accelerated physical development marked by increases in weight and height.

- Mature at varying rates; girls develop earlier than boys.

- Experience irregular growth spurts.

- Have uneven bone-muscle growth, resulting in lack of coordination.

- Are often at a plateau in brain growth and development.

- Experience fluctuations in metabolism that cause extreme fatigue and extreme energy.

- Can be wildly energetic one hour and deeply lethargic the next.

- Lack physical health and have poor levels of endurance, strength, and flexibility.

- Tire easily, but are reluctant to admit it.

- Mostly do not get the 8 to 10 hours per night of sleep they need—limiting their abilities to learn, listen, concentrate, remember information, and solve problems in school.

- Have ravenous appetites including appetites for peculiar tastes; lack good nutritional habits.

- In many cases, tend to lag in needed physical activity, getting less than the one hour a day (at least) that is needed.

- Are self-conscious about learning new physical feats.

- Are disturbed by changes in the body and rate of development.

- Are concerned about their physical development and appearance; worry about being normal physically and sexually.

- Are troubled if they are overdeveloped or underdeveloped physically.

- May display shyness, blushing, or modesty regarding their sexuality.

- Have increased interest in the opposite sex.

- Are chronically concerned about their physical and sexual attractiveness to others.

- Often feel awkward or strange about themselves and their bodies.

Emotionally, young adolescents . . .

- Are easily offended and are sensitive to criticism.

- Focus on self, alternating between high expectations and poor self-concept.

- Are introspective; reflect on their feelings.

- Exhibit erratic emotions and behavior.

- Worry about schoolwork, exams, grades.

- Are moody and restless.

- Often feel self-conscious and alienated.

- Often lack self-esteem.

- Are introspective.

- Are optimistic and hopeful.

- Search for and struggle with sense of identity.

- Strive for a sense of individual uniqueness.

- Are vulnerable to one-sided arguments.

- Exaggerate simple occurrences.

- Believe that personal issues are unique to themselves.

- Want to be independent from authority.

- Need connections to important adults.

- Are emotionally vulnerable.

- Anger easily.

- Often overreact when criticized.

- Are less able to recover from anger or disappointment than when they were younger.

- Enjoy humor.

- Exhibit emotions and emotional responses that are frightening and poorly understood (often these are triggered by hormonal changes).

- May regress to more childish behavior, particularly when stressed.

- Have improved ability to use speech to express their emotions and opinions.

Socially, young adolescents . . .

- Want and need social acceptance from their peers; are constantly concerned with this.

- Desperately want to belong.

- Are highly influenced by peers (everything from behavior and language to tastes in clothing, activities, and music).

- Are highly influenced by pop culture and media messages.

- Are fiercely loyal to peers and to peer group values.

- Use peers and media role models as sources for standards of behavior.

- Are sometimes cruel and insensitive to those outside the peer group or clique.

- May change friends and peer groups often.

- Are searching for identity; experiment with new identities.

- Act rebellious toward parents, but are still strongly dependent on parental values.

- Realize that parents are not perfect; readily identify their faults.

- Show less affection to parents, with occasional rudeness.

- Complain that parents interfere with independence.

- Often act indifferent to adults; may show belligerence.

- Challenge authority figures and test limits of accepted behavior.

- Try out their developing power in various forms (positive and negative).

- Distrust relationships with adults who seem insincere or out of touch with adolescent interests and needs or who show lack of sensitivity to adolescent needs.

- May be argumentative or aggressive.

- Want privileges but avoid responsibility.

- Are enamored with celebrities and take them as role models.

- Like periods of being alone.

- Sense the negative impact of adolescent behavior on parents and teachers.

- Seek love, approval, and reinforcement from adults they admire.

Morally and ethically, young adolescents . . .

- Are idealistic.

- Have a strong sense of fairness.

- Are interested in complex questions and issues.

- Ask broad, unanswerable questions about the meaning of life.

- Depend on the influence of home and church for moral and ethical choices and behaviors.

- Explore the moral and ethical issues that confront them in school lessons, on the media, and in daily interactions with their families and peer groups.

- Experience thoughts and feelings of awe and wonder related to their expanding intellectual and emotional awareness.

- Are impatient with the pace of change.

- Are quick to see flaws in others, especially adults.

- Are slow to admit their own faults.

- Face complex moral and ethical questions that they don't have the maturity to handle.

- Are highly influenced by pop culture and media messages.

Loosely adapted from "Characteristics of Young Adolescents" as published in *This We Believe: Keys to Educating Young Adolescents* (NMSA, 2010)

Needs of Young Adolescents

In the school setting, young adolescents need . . .

- Adults who have a keen awareness of young adolescent development.

- Adults who like them, and who build genuine, appropriate relationships.

- Adults who are real and honest.

- Adults who know and understand their world (their interests, fads, fashions, technology, pop culture, heroes, media, music, etc.).

- Attention and expressions of caring throughout the school.

- Adults who are accessible.

- Adults who help them identify their unique abilities and gifts.

- Multiple experiences to help them feel a sense of belonging.

- Help learning how to plan, organize, and evaluate their own learning.

- To have their personal property and rights respected.

- Order, routine, structure, and fixed responsibility.

- A safe environment free from anxiety, conflict, threat, repression, shame, criticism, and unhealthy competition.

- Assurance that the changes and developments in their lives are normal.

- Assistance in handling peer pressures.

- Consequences that are logical outcomes of their behavior.

- Good nourishment, healthy life practices, and adequate rest.

- Acknowledgement of their passion for technology and use of technology.

- Targeted, specific help learning to analyze and evaluate the benefits, consequences, and dangers of technology—including social media.

- Help learning to distill and deal with the multiple (and often inappropriate) messages from media and pop culture.

- Regular learning experiences that integrate technology.

- Protection from violence (bullying, Internet violations, crime).

- Benefits of clear and positive communication and cooperation between home and school.

- To be asked and allowed to have a voice in their lives and learning.

- Plenty of movement, art, humor, emotion, and music.

- Successes that build competence and confidence and that help to quell their self-doubt.

- Learning activities designed with their physical development in mind.

- Regular opportunities to learn, review, and investigate in cooperation and discussion with other students.

- Regular chances to reflect on and evaluate what and how they learn.

- Learning experiences that are active, engaging, challenging, and relevant.

- Learning experiences that foster independence and individuality.

- Learning experiences delivered in appropriate time chunks.

- Many experiences taking responsibility for their own learning and behavior.

- Plenty of opportunity for exploration, questioning, and creativity.

- Regular feedback that is relevant, helpful, and specific.

- Many chances to learn and practice self-evaluation and peer feedback.

- To discuss big questions of life; to tackle high-level concepts and processes.

- Differentiated learning options and expectations.

- Frequent physical activity.

- To have fun.

- To be pulled out of their self-centeredness by applying their ideas and energies to a wilder world.

Appendix B
Resources Cited and Recommended

Assor, A., Kaplan, H., & Roth, G. (2002). Choice is good, but relevance is excellent: Autonomy-enhancing and suppressing teacher behaviours predicting students' engagement in schoolwork. *British Journal of Educational Psychology, 72*(2), 261–278.

Baenen, J. (2005). *H.E.L.P.: How to enjoy living with a preadolescent.* Westerville, OH: Association for Middle Level Education.

Banas, J. A., Dunbar, N., Rodriguez, D., & Liu, S. (2011). A review of humor in education settings: Four decades of research. *Communication Education, 60*(1), 115–144.

Berdik, C. (2017, February 15). Can virtual reality "teach" empathy? *The Hechinger Report.* Retrieved March 1, 2017 from http://hechingerreport.org/can-virtual-reality-teach-empathy/

Berckemeyer, J. (2013) *Taming the team: How great teams work together.* Chicago, IL: World Book, Inc.

Brookhart, S. M. (2017). *How to give effective feedback to your students.* Alexandria, VA: Association for Supervision and Curriculum Development.

Burkhardt, R. (2009). *Inventing powerful pedagogy: Share. 'steal'. revise. own.* Westerville, OH: Association for Middle Level Education.

Caine, R. N., & Caine, G. (2014). 12 Brain/mind natural learning principles. *Brain/mind natural principles expanded.* National Learning Research Institute. Retrieved March 1, 2017 from http://www.cainelearning.com/wp-content/uploads/2014/04/12-Brain-mind-principles-expanded.pdf

Caine, R. N., & Caine, G. (2015). *Brain/mind learning principles in action.* Thousand Oaks, CA: Corwin Press.

Caissy, G. A. (2002). *Early adolescents: Understanding the 10 to 15 year olds* (2nd ed.). Boston, MA: DaCapo Press.

Campbell, K. (2015). *If you can't manage them, you can't teach them.* Chicago, IL: World Book, Inc.

Caskey, M., & Anfara, V. A., Jr. (2014) Developmental characteristics of young adolescents: Research summary. *Association for Middle Level Education.* Retrieved March 1, 2017 from https://www.amle.org/BrowsebyTopic/WhatsNew/WNDet/TabId/270/ArtMID/888/ArticleID/455/Developmental-Characteristics-of-Young-Adolescents.aspx

Clunies-Ross, P., Little, E., & Kienhuis, M. 2008, Self-reported and actual use of proactive and reactive classroom management strategies and their relationship with teacher stress and student behavior, *Educational Psychology, 28*(6), 693–710.

Comer, J. P. (1995). *Poverty and learning: Nine powerful practices.* Lecture given at Education Service Center, Region 11, Houston, TX.

Common Sense Media. (2012). *Social media, social life: How teens view their digital lives: A Common Sense Media research study.* Retrieved March 1, 2017 from https://www.commonsensemedia.org/research/ social-media-social-life-how-teens-view-their-digital-lives

Common Sense Media (2015a). *The Common Sense census: Media use by tweens and teens.* Retrieved March 1, 2017 from https://www.commonsensemedia.org/research/ the-common-sense-census-media-use-by-tweens-and-teens

Common Sense Media. (2015b). *Landmark report: U.S. teens use an average of nine hours of media per day, tweens use six hours.* Retrieved March 1, 2017 from https://www.commonsensemedia.org/about-us/news/press-releases/ landmark-report-us-teens-use-an-average-of-nine-hours-of-media-per-day

Connors, N. (2014). *If you don't feed the teachers they eat the students: Guide to success for administrators and teachers!* 2nd edition. Chicago, IL: World Book, Inc.

Craig, W. M., & Pepler, D. (2000). Observations of bullying in the playground and in the classroom. *School Psychology International, 21*(1), 22–36.

Cullum, A. (2000). *The geranium on the windowsill just died but teacher you went right on.* Paris, France: Harlin Quist Books.

Cushman, K. (2003). *Fires in the bathroom: Advice for teachers from high school students.* New York, NY: The New Press.

Cushman, K. & Rogers, L. (2009). *Fires in the middle school bathroom: Advice for teachers from middle schoolers.* New York, NY: The New Press.

Deerfield teen saves drowning man, son on Hawaii vacation. (2016, December 27). *ABC News WLS TV.* Retrieved March 1, 2017 from http://abc7chicago.com/news/ deerfield-teen-saves-drowning-man-son-on-hawaii-vacation/1675716/

The drug-like effect of screen time on the teenage brain. (2016, May 4) *PBS Newshour.* Retrieved March 1, 2017 from http://www.pbs.org/newshour/bb/ the-drug-like-effect-of-screen-time-on-the-teenage-brain/

Edwards, S. (2014). *Getting them to talk: A guide to learning discussions in middle grades classrooms.* Westerville, OH: Association for Middle Level Education.

Ehmke, R. (2017). How using social media affects teenagers. *Child Mind Institute.* Retrieved March 1, 2017 from http://childmind.org/article/ how-using-social-media-affects-teenagers/

Ellas, M. (2007, August 16). Never too young to help out. *USA Today*. Retrieved March 1, 2017 from http://usatoday30.usatoday.com/news/nation/2007-08-15-neworleans-teen_N.htm

Erwin, J. (2004). *The classroom of choice*. Alexandria, VA: Association for Supervision and Curriculum Development.

Forni, P. (2003). *Choosing civility: The twenty-five rules of considerate conduct*. New York, NY: St. Martin's Griffin.

Forni, P. (2009). *The civility solution: What to do when people are rude*. New York, NY: St. Martin's Griffin.

Glasser, W. (1999). *Choice theory: A new psychology of personal freedom*. New York, NY: Harper Collins.

Global Nomads Group. (2017). *Global nomads curriculum*. New York, NY: Global Nomads Group. Retrieved March 1, 2017 from http://www.gng.org/vr-lab

Hurren, L. (2010). *Humor in school is serious business*. Chicago, IL: World Book, Inc.

Jackson, R. (2010, September 24). Principle 3 teacher tips: Setting classroom rules. *Mindsteps Blog*. Retrieved March 1, 2017 from: https://mindstepsinc.com/2010/09/setting-classroom-rules/

Jackson, R. (2009). *Never work harder than your students*. Alexandria, VA: Association for Supervision and Curriculum Development.

Kagan, L., Kagan, M., & Kagan, S. (1995). *Classbuilding*. San Juan Capistrano, CA: Kagan Publishing.

Kagan, L., Kagan, M., & Kagan, S. (1997). *Teambuilding*. San Juan Capistrano, CA: Kagan Publishing.

Kagan, S. (2015). *59 Kagan structures*. San Clemente, CA: Kagan Publishing.

Kagan, S. (1992). *Cooperative learning*. San Juan Capistrano, CA: Kagan Publishing.

Kagan, S. (2013). *Kagan Cooperative learning structures*. San Clemente, CA: Kagan Publishing.

Kazakoff, E. R. (2017). *The importance of intrinsic student motivation when selecting educational technologies*. Concord, MA: Lexia Learning.

Lenhart, A. (2012) *Teens, smartphones & texting*. The Pew Research Center Internet & American Life Project. Retrieved March 1, 2017 from http://www.pewinternet.org/2012/03/19/teens-smartphones-texting/

Lenhart, A. (2015). *Teens, social media & technology overview 2015*. The Pew Research Center Internet & American Life Project. Retrieved March 1, 2017 from http://www.pewinternet.org/2015/04/09/teens-social-media-technology-2015/

Lenhart, A., Ling, R., Campbell, S., & Purcell, K. (2010). *Teens and mobile phones.* The Pew Research Center Internet & American Life Project. Retrieved March 1, 2017 from http://www.pewinternet.org/2010/04/20/teens-and-mobile-phones/

Lenhart, A., Purcell, K., Smith, A., & Zickuhr, K. (2010). *Social media & mobile Internet use among teens and young adults.* The Pew Research Center Internet & American Life Project. Retrieved March 1, 2017 from http://www.pewinternet.org/2010/02/03/social-media-and-young-adults-3/

Lenhart, A., Smith, A., Anderson, A., Duggan, M., & Perrin, A. (2015). *Teens, technology & friendships.* The Pew Research Center Internet & American Life Project. Retrieved March 1, 2017 from http://www.pewinternet.org/2015/08/06/teens-technology-and-friendships/

Marzano, R. J., Marzano, J. S., & Pickering, D. J. (2003) *Classroom management that works.* Alexandria, VA: Association for Supervision and Curriculum Development.

Miller, J., & Desberg, P. (2009). *Understanding and engaging adolescents.* Thousand Oaks, CA: Corwin Press.

National Middle School Association. (2010). *This we believe: Keys to educating young adolescents.* Westerville, OH: Author.

The reasons for good manners. (2011, February 12). *Washington Post.* Retrieved March 1, 2017 from http://www.washingtonpost.com/wp-dyn/content/article/2011/02/10/AR2011021005802.html

Ribble, M., & Bailey, G. (2007). *Digital citizenship in schools,* third edition. Eugene, OR, & Arlington, VA: International Society for Technology in Education.

Rideout, V. J., Foehr, U. G., & Roberts, D. F. (2010). *Generation M2: Media in the lives of 8–18-year-olds.* Henry J. Kaiser Family Foundation. Retrieved March 1, 2017 from http://files.eric.ed.gov/fulltext/ED527859.pdf

Robinson, A. (2016, September 19). Fort Wayne teen saves elderly man's life in Walmart. *WANE Nexstar Broadcasting.* Retrieved March 1, 2017 from http://wane.com/2016/09/19/fort-wayne-teen-saves-elderly-mans-life-in-walmart/

Sales, N. J. (2016). *American girls: Social media and the secret lives of teenagers.* New York, NY: Knopf.

Silver, D. (2012). *Fall down 7 times, get up 8: Teaching kids to succeed.* Thousand Oaks, CA: Corwin Press.

Silver, D., Berckemeyer, J., & Baenen, J. (2014). *Deliberate optimism: Reclaiming the joy in education.* Thousand Oaks, CA: Corwin Press.

Spencer, J. (2008). *Everyone's invited! Interactive strategies that engage young adolescents.* Westerville, OH: Association for Middle Level Education.

Strahan, D., L'Esperance, M. & Van Hoose, J. (2001). *Promoting harmony: Young adolescent development and classroom practices.* Westerville, OH: Association for Middle Level Education.

Steiner-Adair, C. (2014). *The big disconnect: Protecting childhood and family relationships in the digital age.* New York, NY: Harper.

Storey, K., Slaby, R., Adler, M., Minotti, J., & Katz, R. (2013). *Eyes on bullying toolkit.* Waltham, MA: Education Development Center, Inc. Retrieved March 1, 2017 from http://www.eyesonbullying.org/pdfs/toolkit.pdf

Summers, J. (2014, August 24). Kids and screen time: What does the research say? *nprEd How Learning Happens. Learning & Tech.* Retrieved March 1, 2017 from http://www.npr.org/sections/ed/2014/08/28/343735856/kids-and-screen-time-what-does-the-research-say

U. S. Department of Education. (2016 December). *Student reports of bullying: Results from the 2015 school crime supplement to the national crime victimization survey.* Retrieved March 1, 2017 from https://nces.ed.gov/pubs2017/2017015.pdf

Van Hoose, J., Strahan, D., & L'Esperance, M. (2009). *Promoting harmony: Young adolescent development and classroom practices.* Westerville, OH: Association for Middle Level Education.

Weissbourd, R. (March 2003) Moral teachers, moral students. *Educational Leadership, 60(6)*, 6–11.

Wolk, S. (2003) Hearts and minds. *Educational Leadership, 61(1)*, 14–18.

Wormeli, R. (2003). *Day one & beyond.* Portland, ME, & Westerville, OH: Stenhouse & Association for Middle Level Education.

Wormeli, R. (2007). *Differentiation: From planning to practice.* Portland, ME, & Westerville, OH: Stenhouse & Association for Middle Level Education.

Wormeli, R. (2001). *Meet me in the middle.* Portland, ME, & Westerville, OH: Stenhouse & Association for Middle Level Education.

Wormeli, R. (2004). *Summarization in any subject: 50 techniques to improve student learning.* Alexandria, VA: Association for Supervision and Curriculum Development.

About the Author
Jack C. Berckemeyer

A nationally recognized presenter, author, and humorist, Jack Berckemeyer began his career as a middle school teacher in Denver, Colorado. After two years of teaching, he was named as an outstanding educator at his school, and shortly thereafter, he was identified as one of the outstanding educators in the district. In 2003, he received the Outstanding Alumni Award from Falcon School District. Jack brings his energy, humor, and expertise about young adolescents to all staff development as he helps teachers and administrators remember why their jobs make a difference.

Jack has presented in conference and school district settings, both nationally and internationally. He served as a judge for the Disney American Teacher Awards and the selection committee for the *USA TODAY* All-Teacher Team. Jack was the assistant executive director for National Middle School Association (now AMLE) for 13 years and co-authored both *HELP for Teachers* and *The What, Why, and How of Student-Led Conferences*. In addition to the original edition and this edition of *Managing the Madness*, he is also the author of *Taming of the Team: How Great Teams Work Together* and co-author of *Deliberate Optimism: Reclaiming the Joy in Education*.

Jack is known for his motivational, practical ideas that bring hope, laughter, and insight about the nature of young adolescents. Jack lives in Denver, Colorado, and has no pets or plants.